CONFLICTS IN SOCIAL SCIENCE

Can social science contribute to the settlement of conflicts while the field is itself divided by intellectual conflicts?

The contributors, while themselves coming from distinct areas of the social sciences, all share the basic assumption that conflicts in social science must be worked out at the level of the individual social scientific disciplines rather than at the level of philosophy. Through a range of detailed case studies, they look at the different ways in which social scientists deal with the tension implied by being at the same time both party to a conflict and a contributor to the settlement of the conflict. They find that at the level of the disciplines there is no unquestioned belief in the conflict-transcending objectivity of the social sciences and that the search for a non-relativistic way of conflict-solving proves to be a subtle and intriguing activity.

Anton van Harskamp is a member of the academic staff at the Centre for the Study of Science, Society and Religion of the Vrije Universiteit in Amsterdam, The Netherlands.

ROUTLEDGE STUDIES IN SOCIAL AND POLITICAL THOUGHT

1 HAYEK AND AFTER
Hayekian Liberalism as a Research Programme
Jeremy Shearmur

2 CONFLICTS IN SOCIAL SCIENCE
Edited by Anton van Harskamp

3 THE POLITICAL THOUGHT OF ANDRÉ GORZ
Adrian Little

CONFLICTS IN SOCIAL SCIENCE

Edited by Anton van Harskamp

ROUTLEDGE

London and New York

First published 1996
by Routledge
11 New Fetter Lane, London EC4P 4EE

Simultaneously published in the USA and Canada
by Routledge
29 West 35th Street, New York, NY 10001

Routledge is an International Thomson Publishing company

Typeset in Garamond by Routledge
Printed and bound in Great Britain by
Biddles Ltd, Guildford and King's Lynn

British Library Cataloguing in Publication Data
A catalogue record for this book is available from the British Library

Library of Congress Cataloguing in Publication Data
Conflicts in Social Science/edited by Anton van Harskamp
p. cm. – (Routledge studies in social & political thought)
Includes bibliographic references and index.
1. Social sciences–Methodology. 2. Social conflict.
I. Harskamp, Anton van, 1946– II. Series
H61.C574 1996
300–dc20 96–2595
CIP

ISBN 0–415–14826–X

CONTENTS

CONTRIBUTORS

P. W. (Bob) Brouwer (1952) is Professor of Law at the Universiteit van Amsterdam. He studied Law and Legal Philosophy in Groningen and Salzburg, and was a Leverhulme Trust Fellow at the Centre of European Governmental Studies, University of Edinburgh (1984–5). He has published *Coherence in Law: An Analytical Study* (1990, in Dutch), and several articles on the problems of legal theory.

André Droogers (1941) is Professor of Cultural Anthropology of Religion at the Vrije Universiteit, Amsterdam. He lectured and did research in Zaire en Brazil. He is the author of four books and numerous articles, and served as co-editor of eight collections, the latest of which, on Pentecostalism in Latin America, will be published by Scarecrow Press in 1996. Between 1991 and 1995 he was president of the Dutch Anthropological Association.

Anton van Harskamp (1946) works at the Interdisciplinary Centre for the Study of Science, Society and Religion of the Vrije Universiteit, Amsterdam. He studied Philosophy and Theology. He was a research fellow and lecturer at the Faculty of Theology at the Katholieke Universiteit Nijmegen and obtained his PhD in 1986. He has published a book on the method of the critique of ideology (in Dutch, forthcoming in German) and several articles on secularization and the sociological analysis of philosophy and theology.

Peter Kloos (1936) read Social Geography and Cultural Anthropology at the Universiteit van Amsterdam, where he obtained his PhD in 1971. He carried out fieldwork in the Netherlands, in Surinam and in Sri Lanka. His publications concerning research outside the Netherlands include *The Maroni River Caribs of Surinam* (Assen: Van Gorcum, 1971), 'The Arikuyo Way of Death' (in: E. Basso ed., *Carib-Speaking Indians*, Tucson: The University of Arizona Press, 1977), *Land Policy and Agricultural Underproduction in a Sinhalese Village in Sri Lanka* (South Asian Anthropologist 9, 1988). He is Professor of Sociology of Non-Western Societies at the Vrije Universiteit, Amsterdam.

Albert W. Musschenga (1950) is Professor of Social Ethics and Director of the Interdisciplinary Centre for the Study of Science, Society and Religion at the Vrije Universiteit, Amsterdam. He has published several books on the foundations of morality and on the concept of quality of life. He is editor of, and contributor to, numerous books on (practical) ethical questions.

Philip Quarles Van Ufford (1939) reads at the Department of Sociology of Development and Anthropology at the Vrije Universiteit, Amsterdam. His current fields of interest are: the development policy practices; the chaos theory; the emptying and destruction of meaning; and the reconstitution of these disciplines as moral sciences. His most recent publication is with R.D. van den Berg (eds) (1995), *De Toekomst van de Nederlandse Ontwikkelingshulp*, Amsterdam: Mets/Agora.

Jan P. Verhoogt (1939) is Senior Member in Political Theory at the Department of Political Science at the Vrije Universiteit, Amsterdam. He has published various articles on the nature and problems of the Dutch welfare state and on the social and moral foundations of modern democracy.

1

CONFLICTS IN SOCIAL SCIENCE

Anton van Harskamp

What is the use of social science? An apparently naïve answer is that social science can contribute to the betterment of society: its systematically verified truth may provide the key to the settlement of disruptive conflicts. To take two random examples: by gaining insight into the cycle of debt and poverty in the Third World, social science is supposed to do its part in helping to find solutions for the conflicts in the Third World; by investigating the causes of child abuse in the nuclear family, it is supposed to do the same in numerous families. The same applies to many more areas of antagonism and conflict. At any rate, this is what many students expect who go to university or college to study social science (Webb 1995: 156ff.).

Are we really dealing with a naïve answer? The authors of this volume presuppose that this is not the case. It is an inherent claim of social science that it can function as one of the (intellectual) tools in the settlement, i.e. closure, management or containment, of social conflicts. Some sociologists even suggest that 'their' science is socially indispensable: given the discordant chaos of groups and social worlds, its theoretical findings not only contribute to mutual understanding, but they also induce us to commitment to rational, non-violent persuasion, which is so badly needed in this irrational and violent world (Berger and Berger 1972: 363).

Even if one does not share this fairly idealistic view, it is still reasonably safe to advance the opinion that the social sciences originally were designated as the most rational way to deal with conflicts in a constantly changing world. The conjunction of events linking the political and socio-cultural thrust of the American and French revolutions to the vast socio-economic changes in the nineteenth century produced the great founding fathers of the social sciences directed at conflicts which were disturbing social order (Laeyendecker 1981; Heilbron 1990; De Wilde 1992). Marx and Engels, for instance, were searching for the explanation of class conflicts; Durkheim was driven by the intuition that the socio-cultural cohesion of nation and state in the French Third Republic was torn apart by individualization and other conflict-conducive processes; Weber was fascinated by the question of why precisely rationalization occurred in a Western context and why it resulted in a 'frozen conflict' between the individual and bureaucratic apparatuses. Despite the differences between these great figures, they devised their theoretical conceptions, either in a direct way (Marx, Engels, etc.) or in a more indirect way (Durkheim), as a means of gaining practical results in a conflict-ridden world. Even Weber, who explicitly recognized conflict as inherent in modern social structure, and who did not subscribe to the idea that social science should have an immediate impact on social policy, was motivated by a personal concern that social science should ultimately contribute to counterbalancing the increasing number of value conflicts in the Western world; conflicts which he considered as consequences of the paradoxical outcome of rationalization: the expansion of irrationality (Albrow 1990: 283ff.; Sica 1990: 13, 101, 195ff.).

THE QUESTION

This brings us up against a problem. Despite the lofty inherent claim of social science that it is supposed to contribute to the settlement of conflicts, the social facts are that the field is heavily torn by intellectual conflicts. The student who intends to study social science with a humanitarian concern will soon find out that any belief in a social scientific truth which could contribute to the settlement of conflicts is lost among a myriad of conflicting theories and interpretations. The most obvious question will then be: *Can social science satisfy its inherent claim to contribute to the settlement of conflicts when the field of social science is divided by conflicts?*

To make the question still more disturbing for the student, intellectual conflicts not uncommonly radiate into the world 'out there'. Some sociologists of science even suggest that the traditional distinctions between science and the world 'out there' are blurred. The German sociologist of science Peter Weingart, for instance, detects a process of de-differentiation between social sciences and public policy-making. It is often unclear whether we are dealing with a conflict in matters of public policy with a social scientific dimension, or with a social scientific conflict with a policy dimension (Weingart 1983: 235). We have only to think of debates concerning the fight against crime, such as those for and against the enlargement of the jurisdiction of investigatory services, not to mention questions relating to immigration control, family planning methods and countless other topics. People always try to defend their own point of view by means of social scientific expert assessment. In this process, numerous social scientists find themselves caught up in an inextricable entanglement of scientific conflicts and societal antagonisms. This all seems to make it even more difficult to live up to the claim of settling conflicts.

A central assertion in this volume is that the question raised by the prospective student is a very serious one. It touches on the self-image and the social credibility of the social sciences. However, it is not uncommon to play down the seriousness of this question. Three relativizing views should be mentioned in this respect: first, that conflict is not a neglected issue in the social sciences but a major field of study; second, that the role played by conflict is not always negative, but often fulfils positive functions in society and the world of science; and, third, that social science is inevitably a conflict-ridden enterprise, which seems to mean that complaints about the occurrence of conflicts are not useful.

The reader will perhaps be surprised, but the authors of this volume endorse these views too. However, we do not think that they can function as a relativization of the question which is at stake here and so let us briefly indicate what these views are and what they entail.

We are well aware of the fact that conflict constitutes one of the most fruitful sources of reflection and ingenuity in the social sciences. The study of conflicts in society is a major stimulus in the refinement and development of the knowledge of social structures and actions (Coser and Larsen 1976). However, we shall argue that, although conflicts are an important object of study, reflective knowledge about conflicts, as far as social scientists are involved, is a wrongly neglected issue in contemporary social research.

We also hold the view that social conflicts, considered as a struggle over values and claims to status, power and resources, can fulfil positive functions. For instance, conflicts can clear the air between competing groups, direct struggling parties to the expression of their own identity, reduce an atmosphere of uncertainty by the maintenance of group boundaries, and stimulate a common search for shared basic assumptions and values or for safety-valve institutions, etc. In short, they may increase rather than decrease the adaptation or adjustment of social relationships or groups (Coser 1964; Stevens 1994). And as far as the finding of facts, theories and basic assumptions in the social sciences is also a socio-cultural process, it is quite sure that conflict can be a positive factor. 'Controversies', writes Helga Nowotny, 'are an integral part of the collective production of knowledge; disagreements on concepts, methods, interpretations and applications are the very lifeblood of science and one of the most productive factors in scientific development' (cited by Mendelsohn 1987: 93). All the same, we are bound to say that not every conflict in science is a productive factor. In particular, the first three chapters in this volume, dealing with conflicts in the field of ethnography and cultural anthropology, refer to conflicts in which the participants find themselves engaged in an almost destructive intellectual trench warfare, while at the same time they realize that the settlement of conflict would mean real progress in their field. We suppose that virtually every social scientist knows of conflicts in his or her field which have reached an anti-productive deadlock.

But – to turn to the third relativizing view – is it not a plain fact that the social sciences are essentially a conflict-ridden enterprise? Are the practitioners in this field not urged to accept that a lot of conflicts cannot be settled at all? We shall argue here that the nature of social science entails the inevitable character of conflict in this field. All social scientists find themselves caught up in a constellation in which not only cognitive arguments but also normative, cultural and social interests are at stake. However, we shall also argue that this may not result in indifference as to the settlement of conflicts. One reason for this is that some conflicts simply must be settled. The more a social scientific discipline is engaged in framing actual decisions in a situation of dispute, the more the practitioner of this discipline feels constrained to take sides in a conflict, and above all at the same time to point to a workable settlement. The last three chapters in this volume are illustrative in this respect: in the field of political science, moral philosophy and legal studies, one generally cannot afford to remain neutral in a conflict, because plausible arguments for a settlement have to be advanced.

What is at stake in this volume, then, is the question of whether social science can satisfy its inherent claim to contribute to the settlement of a conflict, while social scientists are aware that they are a party to the very same conflict.

The reader will notice that this volume displays a Dutch connection. Although the question at stake has a general validity, most case studies are centred on or have their origins in a Dutch context. Perhaps it is even possible to see a Dutch connection in the general stance of the authors in this volume. On the one hand, they all are convinced that conflict is inherent in society, and in so far as science is a socio-cultural process, that conflict is not an intrusion of irrational factors into proper scientific reasoning but is inherent in it. On the other hand, every author is interested in the way in which social science can be a valuable instrument to deal with conflict in a productive and non-violent way. We do not conclude from the inherency of conflicts that a biased partiality in social science is all there is; nor do we infer that the only plausible option left is a detached, melancholic observation of the worldly turmoil. Perhaps our stance is in a certain way induced by a Dutch tradition. Traditionally, the Netherlands is a country in which highly antagonistic religious, ideological and ethnic sections of the population live in close proximity to one another. This seems to foster an attitude in which conflict is openly designated and defined, while all the conflicting parties are convinced that their own conflicts must not be played out to the end, but must be managed and constrained. The system of compartmentalization was once a fine illustration of this attitude (Lijphart 1975). Even the smooth, non-violent yet deep cultural transformation of the Netherlands in the 1960s can be considered as the consequence of a habit which favours the displaying of conflicts within a framework of consensus (Kennedy 1995).

Without attaching too much weight to this conjecture, let us proceed to the question of why precisely conflicts in which social science itself is embroiled deserve our special attention. We consider that recent thinking on the development of science has focused on conflict as a privileged locus for approaching an understanding of the feasibilities of science. Some reasons for this conviction will be given in the following section. However, in particular with regard to the social sciences, we also consider that the question of the prospective student is not really tackled in the existing literature. This is a distinctive characteristic of the present volume, for the answer to the student's question is not provided in the first place by purely theoretical social science nor by the philosophy or sociology of science. The authors are convinced that, if there is a plausible answer at all, it must in the first place be demonstrated by workers in the field at the level of the particular disciplines. We will conclude this introduction with a short summary of the various problems which are tackled in the chapters.

SCIENTIFIC RELATIVIZATION OF SCIENCE?

When one tries to obtain reasoned impressions of recent philosophical and sociological views of the development of science, one soon runs up against paradoxes. It is not unlikely that one of them will be the paradox that the relativization of the social sciences as instruments of conflict settlement is probably increased by the social scientific study of science. In this connection, let us touch on some elements in the recent history of the study of science.

It is no exaggeration to say that Thomas S. Kuhn's *The Structure of Scientific Revolutions* (1970) not only stimulated the historical study of the sciences immensely, but also introduced an entirely new perspective on the phenomenon of science and on the ways in which science is embedded in the always conflict-ridden societal context. In the latter sense, it is justified to think in terms of a period before and a period after Kuhn.

Before Kuhn, the dominant view of science was determined by the conviction that there should be a sharp distinction between the cognitive content of science, its cognitive procedures (methodology) and the focal intellectual norms of the scientist, on the one hand, and the social, economic, political, psychological, even philosophical and religious conditions in which science was produced, on the other hand. According to Barry Barnes, many theories of knowledge were morality plays set in a Manichean cosmos (Barnes 1982: 22). Science in its most ideal expression was imagined as a world of light, as an area of agreement by rational and consensual appeal to facts and validated theories, whereas the real world was supposed to be ruled by irrationality, convention, dogma, and many other figures dressed in black. Only the atmosphere which shaped the conditions in which science was executed was thought to be disfigured by conflicts. Of course, it was known that scientists were always in conflict, but these conflicts were interpreted as having a purely intellectual nature. They were encompassed by the 'ethos of science' which Robert Merton once outlined so impressively (cf. Mulkay 1979: 21ff.). The conflicts and controversies in the world of science were considered as highroads to the overcoming of all conflict, main stimuli to reach out for the one and only truth that will ultimately emerge and prevail.

One of the most decisive influences of *The Structure of Scientific Revolutions* is probably that it made clear that this image of science was basically an idealized one, far removed from the real world of science, for Kuhn undermined the neat demarcation between science and non-science. He demystified the image of a disembodied scientist who, motivated only by the institutional imperatives of science – according to Robert Merton these were universalism, communism, disinterestedness, organised scepticism – functioned as 'a camera, recording truth as a film records an image' (Barnes 1982: 42). Kuhn, however, made it clear that all sorts of social and cultural contingencies were involved in the judgements and inferences of science.

Debates on Kuhn's achievement were above all centred around the well-known concept of 'paradigm'. This concept was heavily criticized by many philosophers because of its indisputable vagueness, and the judgement of Kuhn's critics was corroborated when it became obvious that Kuhn himself was unable to clear up the concept. Nevertheless, the concept has gained its right to exist. This may well be because we have come to realize that the function of this concept is not to designate a certain state of affairs in a clear and distinctive way, but to make us aware of a complex series of questions. 'Paradigm' is a sensitizing concept. It says that, in observing reality, it is neither reality itself nor the meticulous use of methods which determine in the first place which parts of reality we select and which statements are true or false. The concept 'paradigm' tells us that the a priori Gestalt of the set of issues at stake plays a major role in directing groups of scholars towards the identification of these problems and the required methodology. This is particularly the case when a scientific field enters a state of crisis, and scientists and scholars are in conflict with one another about the question of whether the existing theories and methods fit the new phenomena. Investigation of this kind of crisis in the history of science made clear to Kuhn the complex nature of a transition to a new paradigm. These decisive 'developments' in science are not induced by the desire to provide new answers to apparently insoluble questions; they are mainly brought about by a shift in the Gestalt which communities of scientists attach to their particular set of questions.

Two points are important in this respect. In the first place, a paradigm is not a cognitive, but a normative concept: it directs a community of scientists at a pre-scientific level towards their field of study and towards the kind of problems that are prevailing. In that sense, a paradigm delineates in advance the scientific problematic, even what a correct scientific process is, including what criteria are valid in testing hypotheses. In the second place, parts of a paradigm are elements which, according to the traditional image of science, belong to the always conflict-ridden world outside the sciences. A Kuhnian paradigm may comprise not only philosophical views on the fundamental nature of reality, but also the basic normative ideas and concepts which are usually not open to scientific discourse for the simple reason that they themselves are the cornerstones which enable a scientific discourse.

The Structure of Scientific Revolutions was the beginning of a trend in the study of science in which the distinction between the presupposed conflict-free world of science and the conflict-ridden world 'out there' was blurred. A lot of more or less subtle distinctions were used to avoid the seemingly unpleasant consequences for the lofty image of science which Kuhn's way of thinking seems to entail. Most of them were varieties of the distinction between the external and the internal dimensions of science. Some popularity was gained, for instance, by an older distinction between the context of discovery and the context of justification. The former was the sphere in which idiosyncrasies, particular interests, negotiations, power and status, in short all kinds of contingency, including conflicts, were considered as external means by which a group of scientists came about their theoretical findings; the latter was supposed to be a conflict-free sphere in which only facts and sound arguments determined theoretical knowledge. Various philosophers and sociologists of science, however, are telling us today that this distinction cannot be maintained. As far as the concept 'context of justification' implies that it is plain reality which in the last resort determines theoretical knowledge, the concept points to some kind of 'retroactive falsification'. This entails an epistemological denial of the insight that all theoretical knowledge comes down to human interpretation, an insight which involves the inevitability of different and conflicting interpretative views (Goodman 1978). Furthermore, it entails a sociological denial that, at the cognitive level of choice, validation and evaluation, the world of science is – albeit implicitly and mostly without acknowledgement by the profession or after being rendered innocuous by massive qualification – based on the 'normal' mixture of personal, social and political antagonisms (Mendelsohn 1987; Woolgar 1988).

Those who were alarmed by this tendency to undermine the demarcations between science and non-science thought they could detect a dangerous relativistic and self-defeating impulse in thinking about science. At a purely philosophical level, one can understand the grounds for apprehension. Kuhn himself certainly was not and is not a radical relativist. He allows, for instance, some non-conflictual cross-paradigm intelligibility, and he is inclined to think that paradigms are essentially complementary, apparently presupposing that every paradigm brings out some aspects of the world, however partial or minor they may be (Harré and Krausz 1996: 83ff.). Just because of the great but none too subtle visions of Kuhn, however, a radical extrapolation was looming of the vague lines that he had started to sketch, leading to consequences which were devastating with respect to the conflict-solving potential of science. A dangerous point is supposed to be reached whenever the case is made for scepticism: the proposition that, since every 'paradigm' is bound to the particular and changing forms of life, to a specific social tradition, or to the inclinations and tastes of a community of scientists, it is impossible to choose between alternative theories. Conflicts between these theories have to be played out until they fade away for non-epistemic reasons (loss of interest, death, external constraint, etc.). This form of scepticism is bound to lapse into even more radical positions (Weindel 1990: 49ff.). For instance, it may lead to indifferentism concerning the possibility of a scientific search for truth at all, or into the rather cynical stance that, since a rational choice between scientific alternatives is thought to be impossible, one is entitled to present one's own theory as the only valuable theory with all possible means, except of course rational and argumentative ones, while assuming that 'truth' is no more than a rhetorical device that is always subsidiary to particular interests, such as political ones (Devine 1989).

These radical forms of relativism are – again, at a philosophical level – in the last resort self-defeating. They claim that their own viewpoint is true, while undermining the idea that there should be a commitment to truth in science as a regulatory ideal (Phillips 1987: 24; Searle 1994). They try to secure consensus and agreement with their views by saying that conflict and non-agreement is all there is.

At a philosophical level, then, there was some justification for fear of the self-defeating relativizing tendencies in the views on science after Kuhn's *The Structure of Scientific Revolutions*. However, the sceptical forms of relativism which could lead to indifferentism did not cry victory. In other words, it did not bring about the consequence which seems plausible: it did not cause a decline in scientific production or in scientific studies of the world of science.

A remarkable development in the study of science was an empirical turn, which involved a move away from a philosophical study of science towards a more pragmatic stance, generally induced by a historical and sociological approach. This development was remarkable because of the fact that scientists in this field were inclined to some form of epistemological relativism, or, even more radically, to ontological anti-realism, while at the same time they were establishing a new scientific field that is well-respected today: the scientific sociology of science (SSK). One can think, to mention some names, of Karin Knorr-Cetina, Everett Mendelsohn, and the Edinburgh Strong Programme (Barry Barnes and David Bloor). They endorse some form of epistemological relativism. According to them there is no scientific knowledge that is not mediated by the conflict-ridden products of culture, language and representational devices. Scientific institutions, epistemologies and knowledge claims are human products and thus heavily influenced by social forces. These scholars can be called 'mild constructivists' (Sismondo 1993). The epithet 'mild' is applicable because they do not deny the prior existence of the world-as-it-is, the world as an unending stream of material entities and relations. Some mild constructivists are more agnostic or indifferent with respect to the role that the world-as-it-is plays in constituting scientific knowledge claims, while others even acknowledge this role, arguing that we can encounter only limited aspects of it. They all agree that in the reconstruction of scientific processes the view that observation and experiment play the dominant role in the specification of facts and theories is not sustainable, for these processes involve collective negotiations and interests within a community of scientists (Knorr-Cetina 1993: 556). More radical constructivist positions, like those taken in Bruno

Latour's and Steve Woolgar's *Laboratory Life* (1979) or in Woolgar's more recent work, come close to ontological relativism. Their position boils down to the assertion that only conflict-ridden negotiation makes up knowledge. The facts of reality are nothing but an outcome of the collective human constructions. This implies that the objects under study in science do not have a basis in some sort of reality outside the social communities of science. The socially constructed representations simply are those very objects: representation is all there is (cf. Woolgar 1988).

This is not the place to spell out the details of the distinct forms taken by this empirical turn in the study of science. It will suffice to put forward the observation that most studies which are representative of this empirical turn point to the significance of scientific conflicts as material for study. We can give two reasons for this. First, from Kuhn on, conflicts are considered to be the hinge points around which the development as well as the stagnation of science takes place. Second, conflicts are virtually the most fruitful cases from which one can read off the complex interrelationship between the official, institutionalized world of science and the non-scientific world.

SHOW IT!

To return to the central question – Can social science satisfy the inherent claim of settling conflicts if social science itself is embroiled in conflicts? – we do not find much relevant material in the literature. An obvious reason for this is that research on conflicts in science from Kuhn on is directed at the natural sciences, not the social sciences. In 1987 a volume of essays was published in which at first sight the central issue seems to have some affinity with this volume: *Scientific Controversies* (edited by H. T. Engelhardt and A. L. Caplan). The focus of this really impressive volume is the notion of scientific controversy. Moreover, the contributions deal with controversies which have heavy political and ethical ramifications. However, as the subtitle indicates, the volume contains 'case studies in the resolution and closure of disputes in science and technology'. This orientation towards the natural sciences and technology determines one of the major differences from the essays collected in this volume.

This difference has to do with the (im)possibility – whenever a conflict is at stake – of distinguishing neatly between epistemic, i.e. essentially knowledge-based factors, on the one hand, and non-epistemic factors such as personality traits, institutional pressures, political pressures, etc., on the other. Not only are the editors and most of the contributors to *Scientific Controversies* convinced that the closure or resolution of conflicts should mainly be brought about by epistemic factors, but they also believe that in relatively ideal circumstances this will be the case. The distinction between epistemic and non-epistemic factors, as one of the contributors to *Scientific Controversies*, Ernan McMullin, makes clear, should not to be equated with the conventional internal–external distinction, because the latter tends to lend itself too easily to a positivistic exclusion of such non-standard factors as implicit principles of method, or philosophy and worldview (McMullin 1987: 60ff.). The clue here is that 'epistemic' has a broader range than 'internal': 'epistemic' does not only point to factors which in 'normal science' are considered to belong to science, such as observation reports, hypotheses and interpretations, but it also points to factors which usually are not explicitly taken into account because they are implicit or foundational. All the same, they may belong to the realm of well-founded knowledge.

It may well be the case that this distinction makes good sense in the natural sciences, but it will be much more difficult to use it in the social sciences. In his essay in *Scientific Controversies*, McMullin also notes that the distinction bears on the natural sciences alone: '... political and social value differences are often integral to controversy in the social sciences, whereas they must be counted as nonepistemic factors where the natural sciences are concerned' (McMullin 1987: 90 n.60). It probably is no coincidence that *Scientific Controversies* displays some inclination to speak of the 'interplay' of, for instance, knowledge and values, or knowledge and politics, while we consider that, due to the hermeneutic character of the social sciences, words like 'mingling' or 'mixture' are more appropriate. This calls for explanation.

With respect to the object of science, the situation in the social sciences is more complicated than in the natural sciences, because of the plain fact that whenever the object is part of present socio-cultural reality, it is nearly always talking back in a bewildering way. The object of the social sciences is a symbolically structured reality, a world of values, which inevitably means a world full of conflicts of all sorts. We here encounter the well-known 'double hermeneutic' of the social sciences. The concept sounds respectable enough, but it points to a very complex set of problems: the social sciences explore and interpret an object which is exploring and interpreting itself.

In thinking about the significance of the 'double hermeneutic' one encounters a fundamental human predicament: whenever I want to understand another human being, the other cannot be treated like an object whose existence has nothing at all to do with my life. Understanding involves transcending the position of the detached observer. I must try to make the other a part of my perspective, which basically involves the need to widen my perspective, for I have to search for an interpretation in which are merged the other's significance for my particular lifeworld, as well as real otherness. A consequence of this insight is that, if social scientists do not want to force their 'objects' into a straitjacket of general social laws and rules of evidence and inference, reducing them to things without freedom and spontaneity, they inevitably have to adopt a partisan position in the field of exploration, since the self-explorations and self-interpretations of the 'objects' will be related to the more or less open fighting out of conflicts in daily life. In other words, to aim at proper social scientific understanding, and in the last resort to aim for a resolution of (disruptive) societal conflicts by means of that understanding, involves participation into that field of societal conflicts. One cannot avoid siding with a position.

The latter assertion – a consequence of the hermeneutic character of the social sciences – highlights our central question in a certain way. Conflict is not a regrettable intrusion into social science. It is part and parcel of social science itself. We are thus dealing with an intrinsic tension within social science itself – between the claim that social science should function as an intellectual tool in the resolution of a conflict, and the claim that the social scientist takes part in that conflict. As already indicated, there is not much relevant literature on this tension.

To be sure, social theorists certainly draw attention to this tension. Anthony Giddens and Jürgen Habermas, for instance, are aware of the intricate relations between conflicts in science, conflicts in society, and the partisan positions of scientists. However, they do not and will not proceed to the point where we are able to observe empirically the conflict-containing and conflict-solving potential of the social sciences. They only assure us that social science, taken as a discursive intellectual practice, is both aiming at truth and driven forward by an emancipatory interest. On their view, social science is ultimately directed towards universal consensus of opinion, while it inevitably shows partiality in conflict situations (Harbers 1986: 30). Habermas's 'project', for instance, which founds the communicative rationality of the social sciences on an analysis of everyday language, can be considered as an attempt to reinterpret the traditional claims of the social sciences as sciences for social reform, including the closure, containment or management of disruptive conflicts. This attempt, however, is located at the philosophical level of basic ideas, the level where the foundation of the social sciences is supposed to be established. Habermas does not account for clearing up an actual situation in the field of social science in which schools and disciplines, often connected with certain cultural and political biases and interests, form closed fronts against one other – a situation in which there is no communication, but more or less outspoken hostility, usually manifesting itself in a depressing fight for status, students, academic power and financial resources.

In other words, at a meta-level theorists can point to the intrinsic tension within social science, but this does not offer any indication of how the distinct disciplines are supposed to deal with it. To formulate the issue more sharply, they do not themselves take up the issues to which they refer, i.e. the possibility that social science may be torn apart by the claim to solve conflict and the claim to partiality. We, on the contrary, believe that this way of dealing with the two claims is of the utmost importance for the feasibility of social science, not to mention its self-image and social credibility. That is the *first reason* why we consider that what is needed is simply to show in particular cases how social scientific disciplines that are involved in anti-productive and disruptive conflicts can still contribute to solutions, or at least the containment of those conflicts.

In a certain way, the scholars in the tradition of the SSK and of similar scientific approaches to conflict in science do not really take up the issue of our volume either. This is basically because they situate themselves outside the conflicts that they are investigating.

Let us first cast another quick glance at the volume *Scientific Controversies*. The contributions deal with controversies from the past, even though sometimes a very recent past, and the volume focuses on the question of which kind of factors (scientific or non-scientific) once determined the closure of a conflict between two competing parties. In this volume, on the other hand, we are dealing mainly with very recent conflicts and, more importantly, with conflicts in which the scientists who describe them are also involved, in particular because their own normative interests are at stake in those very conflicts.

A similar state of affairs can be found in the SSK tradition. The Dutch philosopher Hans Radder has made it clear that the social constructivists of the SSK are acutely aware of the normative presuppositions and assumptions which so often determine the closure of a scientific controversy. Their method in many of their case studies is a deconstructive critique. However, apparently due to their – at least epistemological – relativism, they are also inclined to consider themselves as genuinely disinterested researchers. This explains the almost total absence of normative reflection within constructivist studies of science and technology (Radder 1992). In other words, the SSK scholars remain outside the conflicts they are describing, in particular outside the normative dimensions of those conflicts.[1]

The interesting point here is that these scholars strongly disclaim the value-free, disinterested attitude and the privileged cognitive status traditionally attached to science, including the ascribed claims to overcome conflicts inside and outside the world of science. Yet at the same time they are producing 'normal science'. They bring their findings before the forum of experts and ask for consensual intersubjectivity, as all traditional truth-seeking science does. They thus relativize science by showing that science itself is riddled by normative conflicts, whereas in fact they uphold the traditional conflict-transcending claims of science.

The conditions which allow this stance all boil down to the intellectual activity of scientifically observing the scientific observers. By observing the ways in which scientists observe reality and by describing the impact of the so-called non-scientific factors, including the ways in which these scientists take part in or even exacerbate conflicts by normative positions, they themselves escape the pressure of the tension which is at stake here: the tension between a conflict-ridden science and the inherent claim of science to overcome conflicts. The German theoretical sociologist Niklas Luhmann has made this insight concerning the effect of observing the observers into one of his central theses about the interrelation of the sciences (Luhmann 1990: 99ff.). According to him, science as a truth-seeking intellectual activity is caught up in a mechanism by which, whenever a scientific discipline is confronted with a fundamental contradiction, say an apparently insoluble conflict, the deeper reasons for this contradiction are explained by another scientific discipline. By understanding, i.e. by describing and explaining why a scientific field cannot solve a problem, the problem ceases to exist, but this is strictly from a perspective which is part of another discipline.

However, if one chooses to stay at the level of a particular science, the tension is not solved at all. No scientific discipline can justify its claim to strive for consensus seriously if it knows at the same time that it is heavily characterized by or even contributes to real conflicts. No discipline can leave the solution of this tension up to a different discipline. That is the *second reason* why the authors of this volume consider that what is needed now is a demonstration of the ways in which particular disciplines are dealing with conflicts.

We conclude this section by giving a *third reason*. It bears on the concept of 'incommensurability', a concept which is often mentioned with respect to those all too familiar anti-productive conflicts within the world of social science.

Generally speaking, a relation between two positions can be called incommensurable when both constitute a discordant situation and supporters of both positions are not willing to acknowledge any objective foundation as a middle ground, say as the basis for a criterium to validate both positions. It has become common practice to use the concept with respect to all sorts of antagonisms: worldviews, lifestyles, language games, research programmes, styles of thinking, paradigms, scientific theories, etc. In this book we target conflicts between convictions, both at the theoretical level of certain social scientific disciplines (cultural anthropology, law studies, political science, ethics) and at the level of the (professional) practice with which these conflicts are frequently connected (ethnography, jurisdiction, politics, morality).

Richard J. Bernstein has introduced a useful distinction with regard to the nature of 'incommensurability' (1983: 82ff.). He calls for a careful distinction between incompatibility, incommensurability and incomparability. The concept of incompatibility is a logical one.[2] Two positions, say two statements, are incompatible whenever there is a common framework, which makes it clear that we are dealing with a real contradiction. A simple example is the statement 'the cover of this book is red' versus 'the cover of this book is grey'. Two statements can be said to be incomparable when there is no relation at all, either with respect to denotation or with respect to the denotated object. For example: 'the cover of this book is red' versus 'the jockey weighs 60 kilos'. The concept of incommensurability has to be located in between these two concepts. This means that, once we have established that the relations in a particular conflictual situation cannot be characterized in terms of incompatibility or incomparability, we can be pretty sure that we are confronted with incommensurability.

After establishing incommensurability, the real work still has to be done. Of course, at a philosophical level one can get lost in ongoing debates concerning the epistemological questions of whether incommensurability is possible at all, whether it boils down to the underdetermination of theory choice by rational arguments, what scope rationality has in a conflict situation, etc. (Laudan 1990: 121ff.). In our view, however, the concept of incommensurability implies that although a plain logical solution to a conflict does not seem attainable because we may not presume an overarching framework, we are still required to try to find a solution (Calhoun 1992). One has to dig deeper than logic – into the level of political or religious values, for example. If a conflict cannot be identified as basically a case of incompatibility or incomparability, we have to presuppose the existence of transitions between the competing parties; we have to set a 'transitional reason' ('transversale Vernunft': Welsch 1995) into action, not in the first place in philosophy or social theory, but in specific cases. In other words, like the concept 'paradigm', the concept 'incommensurability' is a sensitizing concept. It appeals against the tendency to resign ourselves to the fate of closed fronts and the intellectual trench warfare that so often characterize conflicts inside and in relation to the social sciences.

The point at stake should be clear by now. First, incommensurability has to be demonstrated in specific cases. Second, it calls for digging deep and for creative solutions, for non-standard transitions between conflicting thoughts and theories, especially when social scientists find themselves involved with one particular side in a conflict situation.

THE CONTRIBUTIONS

The fact that this book contains contributions from distinct social scientific disciplines is a consequence of our basic assumption: incommensurable conflicts must be worked out at the level of the disciplines. The general purpose of this volume is to observe the different ways in which scientists from distinct disciplines deal with the tension implied by being both party to a conflict and contributor to the settling of that conflict.

The authors feel that the problems they are dealing with are part of a set of issues that goes beyond relativism. They tentatively suppose that the basic assumptions on which relativism is usually founded, such as the social nature of science, the loss of the privileged cognitive status of science, and the fading away of clear-cut boundaries between science and the conflict-ridden world 'out there', do not relieve them of the obligation to practise good science. They presume that these insights do not have to lead to the depressing conviction that every scientist is locked up in a paradigmatic framework – which would render superfluous any contribution to the solution of a conflict – nor to endless philosophical reflexivism.

The first three chapters are concerned with the fields of ethnography and cultural anthropology, while the last three chapters are arranged according to the principle that, the more a discipline is enlisted in framing actual decisions in a situation of dispute, the greater the tension is between the inevitable partiality of a scientist and the need to provide a solution. We could also say that the chapters are arranged according to the degree to which they are expected to provide answers to burning problems in society.

Stephan Fuchs has advanced the thesis that fields like ethnography and cultural anthropology are tending towards relativistic and reflexive positions because they are less routinized in theories, rules of evidence and inference than most other social scientific disciplines. They display a large variety of fairly autonomous schools and worldviews. According to Fuchs, scientists in these fields are often more attracted to hermeneutic questions, to the word and its interpretation, than to the world and its explanation by an appeal to the facts of reality (Fuchs 1992: 161).

Generally speaking, Fuchs' thesis may be true. The interesting point, however, is that the first three chapters in this volume display considerable differences concerning both the extent to which each is willing to accept real conflicts and real disagreements, and the specific ways in which one deals with real conflicts. We recommend the reader to pay attention to the way in which the context of the problem at stake induces each author to identify that problem as more or less pressing.

Philip Quarles van Ufford starts his chapter with a sketch of an intellectual debate in which he was once involved. The debate concerned the complex relationship between a Dutch religious denomination (the Reformed Churches in the Netherlands) and churches in Java, Indonesia. The two antagonists were involved in this relationship, the author himself as a social scientist, his opponent as a policy-maker. The point of this sometimes heated debate was the divergence of interpretation of the policy process in which the relations between the churches were once developed. In reflecting on the course taken by the debate, the author concludes that in the end the two antagonists did not come to any agreement; there was not even agreement on the relevant and verifiable facts. All the same, both he and his opponent felt something had been gained by the debate. The author is trying to grasp the remarkable fact that the cognitive content of a conflict may still exist after the existential heat of the conflict has gone and, above all, when the social dynamics of the conflict point to new investigations and new reflections.

While Quarles van Ufford is inclined to accept that at a cognitive level a conflict concerning the interpretation of a historical process remains unsolved, the next author, *Peter Kloos*, chooses an approach which seems to require a more far-reaching rapprochement of the parties in disagreement. The issue is the phenomenon of multiple images of ethnic reality, and in particular the conflicting descriptions of the same ethnic identities within the same society and culture by different ethnographers. Kloos illustrates his argument with striking examples, most of them outlined as a form of research called ethnographical restudy. He points out several factors which create differences between fieldworkers. On further research most factors appear to be open for objectification, i.e. for a detached presentation on which both conflicting parties basically can reach some agreement. This means that, as far as these kinds of factors are concerned, a conflict can be resolved in a relatively easy way. Real difficulties arise, however, from the factor of 'theoretical research perspective': it is hard for a fieldworker to objectify his or her own research perspective and to understand that of the opponent. Kloos then argues extensively in favour of the integration of metatheorizing into anthropological studies. The motivation behind his argument is political: ethnographic discrepancies can no longer be seen as a purely academic issue. As socially and politically constructed identities, the images of ethnicities can acquire a sinister reality. At first sight metatheory cannot do much about this, for metatheory does not claim to provide an immediate solution for a conflict; it neither devises an all-encompassing framework, nor does it pass judgement for or against one of the parties. However, in bringing out the underlying theoretical foundations of a conflict, it leaves the cognitive content of a conflict unaltered but recognized. Kloos obviously hopes that this metatheoretical recognition of the conflict will be helpful in ending the intellectual trench warfare between anthropological research schools.

The third chapter is by anthropologist *André Droogers*, a scholar in the field of the anthropology of religion. He begins by referring to two fieldwork experiences, both of which called into question the discourse of 'normal' science, in particular the neat and strict boundaries between a religious and a social scientific perspective. These experiences suggested an element of playfulness in both religion and the adequate social scientific perspective. This suggestion leads the author to attempt to transcend a well-known methodological conflict in ethnography which has reached a deadlock for some time. This is the conflict between reductionism and religionism: while the former explains religion entirely by non-religious factors, the latter does not rule out the occurrence of the 'other' reality a priori. The transcendence of this conflict also involves the choice between methodological atheism, agnosticism and theism. As a Christian social scientist, Droogers is motivated to transcend this conflict. His development of the notion of methodological ludism sheds new light on the conflict. Methodological ludism is defined as the capacity to deal simultaneously and subjunctively with two or more perspectives. This contribution provides evidence of the fact that what at first sight appears to be predominantly a purely theoretical and academic conflict which does not urgently require a solution, may turn out to be a conflict which insistently calls for an all-encompassing perspective. The 'explanation' is that this conflict between theoretical research perspectives is at the same time also a conflict within the fieldworker and anthropologist him/herself.

The next chapter is in the field of political science. Political scientist *Jan P. Verhoogt* describes a problem of conflicting loyalties within the majority of the Dutch electorate. It concerns the tension between loyalty to the policy of the Dutch welfare state, which has acquired some reputation as a proper manifestation of the principles of democracy, and a latent leaning to anti-democratic and nationalist counterforces which has not yet found political or institutional expression. Verhoogt reads this tension from a recent poll which concludes that, although the following of a Dutch extreme right-wing party is relatively small, the majority of the Dutch electorate nevertheless accepts the central theme (obsession) of that party as being the most pressing item in society: in other words, these people feel alarmed by the growth and influence of ethnic minorities. The task which the political scientist Verhoogt sets himself is to reconstruct this conflict at the level of political theory by a critical analysis of the complex relationship between abstract principles of democracy and historically defined national communities. He touches briefly on the origins and nature of the European nation-state in order to formulate the Lockean and Rousseauian view of the contradictory but at the same time necessary relationship between principles of democracy and national communities. Verhoogt then points out that in nineteenth-century political theory this relationship was redefined by neglecting the latter in the name of the former. As the policy of the Dutch welfare state was deeply influenced by this theory, this may explain its bias in favour of extending political and social democracy while at the same time undermining the nature and unity of the Dutch national community, which aroused anti-democratic and national counterforces. Verhoogt emphasizes that instead of violating it, we should try to live with the contradictory relationship between abstract principles of democracy and historically defined national communities. This contribution seems to form a classic model of social scientific conflict-solving. Nevertheless, it is not a propensity for classical answers that leads Verhoogt to these alarming tendencies, but the fact that the problem at stake is one the scientist himself experiences as a citizen, and one which is felt to be very pressing by the majority of the Dutch electorate. The nature of this conflict, then, does not allow a social scientist to leave the cognitive content of the conflict unaltered. The scientist is forced to come down in favour of a particular political position.

The following chapter presents a comparable case. The author, *Albert W. Musschenga*, works in the field of philosophical ethics. Because of the fact that not every moral disagreement insistently calls for a solution, Musschenga begins by providing some conceptual clarifications with regard to the question of when we really encounter a pressing moral conflict. The subsequent argumentation takes its starting point in a fictitious conflict. This conflict can be considered as an intensification of possible difficulties occurring in a multicultural society. The issue is whether the regular beating of a fourteen-year-old son by his Moroccan father – a form of behaviour held to be legitimate within the father's cultural context – should be interpreted as a form of punishment or as a form of child abuse. Convinced that moral beliefs are related to particular cultural contexts, respecting persons of all cultures, and knowing that the father is acting rationally and honestly in terms of his own context (a strict version of Moroccan Islam), the author argues that the conflict basically boils down to the question of whether one is morally justified to take measures against the father that could result in enforced removal of the father's parental authority. Musschenga first tackles this problem at the level of meta-ethics, exploring the question of whether a rational solution is conceivable. The conclusion of his subtle argument is that the main theories in the field of meta-ethics, viz. absolutism and relativism, are consistent and plausible. They both claim the possibility of a rational solution. However, since they are also incommensurable, one feels compelled to appeal to the beliefs of one's own moral tradition. In Musschenga's case this is explicitly defined as liberalism. He explores the liberal manner of resolving conflict and the basic assumptions and claims of liberalism, finally concluding that in a case like this liberalism has to be considered as a form of fideism, which is at odds with the dominant liberal self-interpretation. In this contribution the author clarifies first that it is precisely for moral reasons that a decision cannot be evaded – a communicative rationality here runs up against its limits. Second, one of the main functions of ethical reflection in cases like this proves to be the intuition or the cognitive recognition of the inevitability of a bad conscience. This may be helpful if one feels that the conflict cannot be superseded and one still has to take sides.

In the last chapter the urge to find a solution is even more pressing. This chapter, written by *P. W. Brouwer*, is engaged in a field where the philosophy of law and law studies refer to each other.[3] This implies that the reasons for making a decision are induced not only morally, but also legally and juridically. In this field there often is a direct obligation to make a real choice in a conflict, for the set of problems at issue is delivered by the judicial court to the scholar.[4] Brouwer takes as his starting point the criminal prosecution in a Dutch court of a radical evangelical lay preacher, L. Goeree. He was charged with and sentenced for publicly offending a group of people because of their religion. In 1985 he and his wife had published and distributed an article in a magazine in which they expressed in a blunt and shocking way their repugnant anti-Semitic religious conviction: that the Jewish people themselves were held responsible for the sufferings they had endured through the centuries, including the holocaust. Brouwer begins by distinguishing a number of conflicts in order to focus on the central question: given a framework of basic rights, particularly the freedom of speech and the freedom of religion, and the indisputable public offence of a considerable group of people, and given moreover the hermeneutic insight into the inevitability of a personal judgement, is it possible to conceive the outline of a real judgemental impartiality and objectivity of a court of law? After a discussion of all the relevant pros and cons in the Goeree case, he concludes that none of these factors is decisive. This leads him to explore some basic views on the concept of objectivity with regard to a judicial procedure. At first sight his conclusion may appear trivial, but it is in fact a remarkable one. Founding his thesis on awareness of the fact that a judgement is inevitably a human construction, he develops a subtle argument in favour of trying to reach a judicial compromise. In a constitutional state one may expect a certain willingness to accept the creating of objectivity, which in the case at hand results in a compromise.

These chapters provide evidence that conflict-solving at the level of the disciplines is not obsessed by the dilemma of objectivism and relativism. The fact that in a situation of conflict an appeal to an objective foundation which holds independently of the view of the conflicting parties is actually impossible does not lead to some sort of self-defeating relativism. However, both horns of this dilemma are evaded in distinct ways. There simply is no self-indulgent and unquestioned belief in the conflict-transcending objectivity of the social sciences. The ways the authors try to overcome the self-defeating consequences of relativism are rather different. The desire to transcend a specific conflict appears to be dependent on the degree to which a discipline is involved in an actual conflict outside the walls of the academic community. Ranging from a plea for a thoroughly communicative rationality via a plea for integration of meta-theorizing into the disciplines, and via favouring the play of methodological perspectives to distinct forms of taking sides within a conflict, the search for a non-relativistic way of conflict-solving proves to be a subtle and intriguing activity.

NOTES

1 A consequence of radical constructivism in SSK seems to be the acknowledgement that its own discourse is always constructed, contingent and normative. This consequence is taken in Malcolm Ashmore's *The Reflexive Thesis: Wrighting Sociology of Scientific Knowledge* (1989). Ashmore turns the reflective sociology of science into a special version of deconstructionist literary criticism. He defends in a playful and unexpected way the social nature of all science, claiming that all scientific writing is fiction, simultaneously showing that reflexive scientific writing (a sort of meta-fiction) is a fruitful and self-revealing intellectual activity. His concluding chapter takes the form of a fictive oral examination, inviting the reader to make (wright! *sic*) his or her own text: a radical extrapolation of relativistic premises, blurring the institutionally determined boundaries between scientific disciplines and between science and non-science (cf. Fuchs 1992).

2 There are more distinctions regarding the concept of 'incommensurability'. For instance, Bernstein himself refers to Gerald Doppelt who distinguishes, with respect to Kuhn's paradigms, between evaluative standards and problems on the one hand and meanings on the other, suggesting that incommensurability between paradigms can only be applied to the former categories, thereby implying that incommensurability is not to be equated with a fully fledged theoretical division between the paradigms. While Doppelt refers to paradigms in the natural sciences, David Wong chooses a broader scope (Wong 1989). He introduces three versions of the incommensurability thesis concerning overarching cultural 'theories of the world'. Through an ascending order in terms of the intellectual challenge, he first distinguishes incommensurability with respect to translation, which implies that terms in one theory cannot be equated in meaning and reference with terms in the other theory. Second, he points to incommensurability with respect to justification, which means that fundamental premises about the nature of the world or fundamental forms of reasoning are

essentially different. The third version concerns evaluative incommensurability: the claim that it is impossible to make a judgement of superiority between one's own theory and other theories. These two kinds of distinction advanced by Doppelt and Wong, different as they apparently are, are concerned with the question of which theoretical 'objects' are incommensurable. The distinction which is at stake in this introductory chapter, however, designates the concept of incommensurability as a hermeneutic concept.

3 It may not be conventional to classify these kind of studies among the social sciences, but in so far as the social sciences explore the various ways in which human relations are regulated, and law and jurisprudence are major instruments in performing that regulation, we think this classification legitimate.

4 This indicates a rather unique feature in the world of science. While in most social scientific disciplines differences prevail in intellectual practices between academic and non-academic contexts, one may assume that when both a court of law and an academic jurist are studying a specific case, the essential differences between the two activities will not touch on the intellectual aspects, including language, concepts and arguments.

REFERENCES

Albrow, M. (1990) *Max Weber's Construction of Social Theory*, London: Macmillan.

Ashmore, M. (1989) *The Reflexive Thesis: Wrighting Sociology of Scientific Knowledge*, Chicago: University of Chicago Press.

Barnes, B. (1982) *T.S. Kuhn and Social Science*, London: Macmillan.

Berger, P. L. and Berger, B. (1972) *Sociology: A Biographical Approach*, New York: Basic Books.

Bernstein, R. J. (1983) *Beyond Objectivism and Relativism*, Cambridge MA: Blackwell.

Calhoun, C. (1992) 'Culture, History and Specificity', in S. Seidman and D. G. Wagner (eds) *Postmodernism and Social Theory: The Debate over General Theory*, Cambridge MA: Blackwell, 55–83.

Coser, L. A. (1964) *The Functions of Social Conflict*, New York: The Free Press.

Coser, L. A. and Larsen, O. N. (eds) (1976) *The Uses of Controversy in Sociology*, New York: The Free Press.

Devine, P. E. (1989) *Relativism, Nihilism and God*, Notre Dame: Notre Dame University Press.

De Wilde, R. (1992) *Discipline en legende: De identiteit van de sociologie in Duitsland en de Verenigde Staten 1870–1930*, Amsterdam: Van Gennep.

Engelhardt, H. T. and Caplan, A. L. (eds) (1987) *Scientific Controversies: Case Studies in the Resolution and Closure of Disputes in Science and Technology,* Cambridge: Cambridge University Press.

Fuchs, S. (1992) 'Relativism and Reflexivity in the Sociology of Scientific Knowledge', in G. Ritzer (ed.) *Metatheorizing*, London: Sage, 151–67.

Goodman, N. (1978) *Ways of Worldmaking*, Hassocks: The Harvester Press.

Harbers, H. (1986) *Sociale wetenschappen en hun speelruimte*, Groningen: Wolters-Noordhoff.

Harré, R. and Krausz, M. (1996) *Varieties of Relativism*, Cambridge MA: Blackwell.

Heilbron, J. (1990) *Het ontstaan van de sociologie*, Amsterdam: Prometheus.

Kennedy, J. C. (1995) *Nieuw Babylon in aanbouw: Nederland in de jaren zestig*, Amsterdam: Boom.

Knorr-Cetina, K. (1993) 'Strong Constructivism – from a Sociologist's Point of View: A Personal Addendum to Sismondo's Paper', *Social Studies of Science* 23: 555–63.

Kuhn, T. S. (1962, 1970) *The Structure of Scientific Revolutions*, Chicago: University of Chicago Press.

Laeyendecker, L. (1981) *Orde, verandering, ongelijkheid: Een inleiding tot de geschiedenis van de sociologie*, Amsterdam: Boom.

Latour, B. and Woolgar, S. (1979) *Laboratory Life: The Social Construction of Scientific Facts*, London and Beverly Hills: Sage.

Laudan, L. (1990) *Science and Relativism: Some Key Controversies in the Philosophy of Science*, Chicago: University of Chicago Press.

Lijphart, A. (1975) *The Politics of Accommodation: Pluralism and Democracy in the Netherlands*, Berkeley CA: University of California Press.

Luhmann, N. (1990) *Die Wissenschaft der Gesellschaft*, Frankfurt a. M.: Suhrkamp.

McMullin, E. (1987) 'Scientific Controversy and its Termination', in H. T. Engelhardt and A. L. Caplan (eds) *Scientific Controversies*, Cambridge: Cambridge University Press, 49–91.

Mendelsohn, E. (1987) 'The Political Anatomy of Controversy in the Sciences', in H. T. Engelhardt and A. L. Caplan (eds) *Scientific Controversies*, Cambridge: Cambridge University Press, 93–124.

Mulkay, M. (1979) *Science and the Sociology of Knowledge*, London: George Allen & Unwin.

Phillips, D. C. (1987) *Philosophy, Science, and Social Inquiry: Contemporary Methodological Controversies in Social Science and Related Applied Fields of Research*, Oxford: Pergamon Press.

Radder, H. (1992) 'Normative Reflexions on Constructivist Approaches to Science and Technology', *Social Studies of Science* 22: 141–73.

Searle, J. (1994) 'Rationality and Realism: What is at Stake?', in J. R. Cole, E. G. Barber and S. R. Graubard (eds) *The Research University in a Time of Discontent*, Baltimore: Johns Hopkins University Press, 55–83.

Sica, A. (1990) *Weber, Irrationality and Social Order*, Berkeley CA: University of California Press.

Sismondo, S. (1993) 'Some Social Constructions', *Social Studies of Science* 23: 515–53.

Stevens, J. (1994) *In harmonie én conflict: Een multidisciplinaire benadering*, Averbode: Altiora & KBS.

Webb, K. (1995) *An Introduction to Problems in the Philosophy of Social Sciences*, London: Pinter.

Weindel, H. J. (1990) *Moderner Relativismus*, Tübingen: Mohr.

Weingart, P. (1983) 'Verwissenschaftlichung der Gesellschaft – Politisierung der Wissenschaft', *Zeitschrift für Soziologie* 12, 3: 225–41.

Welsch, W. (1995) *Vernunft: Die zeitgenössische Vernunft und das Konzept der transversalen Vernunft*, Frankfurt a. M.: Suhrkamp.

Wong, D. B. (1989) 'Three Kinds of Incommensurability', in M. Krausz (ed.) *Relativism: Interpretation and Confrontation*, Notre Dame: Notre Dame University Press, 140–58.

Woolgar, S. (ed.) (1988) *Knowledge and Reflexivity: New Frontiers in the Sociology of Knowledge*, London: Sage.

2

REALITY EXISTS

Acknowledging the Limits of Active and Reflexive Anthropological Knowledge

Philip Quarles van Ufford

> The tension between universalism and relativism . . . poses a false dichotomy and is unwarranted: we face a situation in which similarity and difference are simply two sides of the same coin, the examination of each necessary to the total analysis.
>
> (A. L. Epstein 1992: 19)

The reflections in this essay explore the theme of the mutual relevance of scientific anthropological knowledge and practical understanding. I sketch and analyse in some detail a singular case of conflicting views which led to a direct confrontation and debate some years ago. The case study gives rise to some questions concerning the evident disparity between insights I had gained after a number of years of research in Central Java and of those of a highly informed insider.

Broadly, the argumentation runs as follows. After sketching the 'unresolved battle' for a shared view of a particularly critical episode in the relationship between an Indonesian church and its Dutch missionary partners, I raise the question why it is that I seemed to have nevertheless benefited from the dispute. After the rather heated encounter, lasting for some hours, at which other people were also present, no agreement concerning the 'relevant and verifiable facts' had been reached. Yet, this seemed not to matter so much anymore. What was gained?

This then leads me to a number of questions concerning the nature of 'reliable' anthropological knowledge. I shall argue that the explicit acknowledgement of *contingency* of academic anthropological understanding constitutes an important dimension of its value and indeed its very claims of scientific 'truth'. An important feature of contingency is situatedness. In this essay I link the contingency of understanding to two specific domains. Firstly to the agora, the ancient Greek city's market place, the public space which citizens, whatever their profession or engagement, from time to time enter and exchange their views. Secondly to the 'churchyard', as the place where the acknowledgement of contingency of our scientific and political modes of understanding is linked to religious understanding and, indeed, to faith. These points of view will lead me back to the case study which will now be presented.

THE CASE: A 'MISUNDERSTANDING' REGARDING MISSIONARY RESPONSIBILITY

Some years ago Dr D.C. Mulder, then Professor of Missions in the Theology Department of the Free University, Amsterdam, wrote to me at length to say that an article of mine had shocked and angered him (Quarles van Ufford 1987). My sketch of the background and intentions of the new policy for Dutch missions to Javanese churches as implemented at the end of the 1960s, he said, was completely wrong.

> You claim that the GKN-Mission (Mission of the Reformed Churches of the Netherlands) acted out of self-interest only. I find this most unfair.... It saddens me to see that you made these unreasonable statements. They're in black and white and likely to stick. I do hope that you are willing and able to correct the picture in subsequent writings.
>
> (letter Mulder, 3 May 1987)

This stern reprimand touched me to the quick. First, because I had, and have, the highest regard for Dr Mulder. Secondly, he had been involved, more than anyone I can think of, with the very mission work I had written about. If anyone knew the history of the relation between the Dutch and the Javanese churches it was he, both academically and perhaps even more important through direct, personal involvement. After 1950 he spent a number of years in the theological department at Yogyakarta and throughout the two decades covered by my article his participation in the mission had been intensive and varied. During the 1970s Dr Mulder was responsible for implementation of the new Dutch mission policy towards the church of Central Java. In short, he was thoroughly familiar with the ins and outs of Dutch mission work on Java and in a unique position to form a detailed picture of intentions and 'interests'. All of this, of course, added great weight to his judgement.

Well, I wrote in reply and some time later we met to discuss the matter at length, finding that, though we agreed on many 'facts' and even on at least one major interpretative framework to place them in, our conclusions remained disparate.

My article dealt with Revd Basuki Probowinoto, an Indonesian church leader who died in 1986. The article appeared in an Indonesian volume dedicated to his life and work. From 1942 onwards, Revd Probowinoto had been one of the most prominent figures in the church of Central Java and beyond that on the nation-wide ecclesiastical scene. As the struggle for Indonesian independence progressed and intensified, Probowinoto's role took on growing importance. As a young pastor in Jakarta he was active in politics and co-founder of Parkindo, the Indonesian Christian party.

My analysis centred on the dilemma which shaped Probowinoto's life and work from 1942 to 1970. The dilemma was as follows:

1 As Indonesian, Probowinoto was a nationalist, opposed to restoration of the old colonial relationships. He took active part in the political struggle against the Dutch.
2 As pastor in the church of Central Java he did not want to break with the reformed churches in the Netherlands. His church owed its existence to their mission work, and Probowinoto thought it vitally important that the bond between his own church and the reformed churches in the Netherlands continue. He defended this view even though many of the Reformed in Holland were unhappy with an Indonesia hankering after independence.

Revd Probowinoto, I wrote, lived with this dilemma for more than thirty years. As a pastor with nationalist leanings he was active in national politics from 1942 to 1950; subsequently, he assumed a primarily ecclesiastical task in Central Java when he became a key figure in the renewed cooperation between the Reformed mission and his church. Throughout, he remained true to both loyalties. During the struggle for independence, from 1948 to 1950, he had put his reputation as Indonesian nationalist at stake. For even then he was an outspoken advocate of post-independence ecclesiastical cooperation between the Netherlands and Java. Many of his fellow church leaders in Yogyakarta, centre of the Indonesian nationalist movement, felt most uncomfortable with Probowinoto's stance; he persisted nonetheless.

Some twenty years later the Reformed mission terminated the ecclesiastical cooperation into which Probowinoto had put so much effort and in support of which had taken considerable personal risk during the struggle for Indonesian independence. To the Indonesian Christians the move came suddenly, virtually without consultation, and took Probowinoto and many others completely by surprise.

In my essay I called this a 'tragic event' – tragic because Probowinoto and others had been put aside 'just like that'. I don't mean to say that there were no good reasons for discontinuing the cooperation. There undoubtedly were. The tragedy was that the Javanese partners had no voice in the decision.

This apparently abrupt, one-sided decision could only be understood against the background of changes on the Dutch ecclesiastical scene and the concomitantly shifting image of 'the' problem in the Javanese church. To church-going folk in the Netherlands, older perspectives on missions and former frameworks of cooperation were losing their attractiveness. Towards the end of the 1960s the leadership of the Reformed mission sought to infuse the mission concept with a new content. It was in this context that I wrote of the mission's 'self-interest' overruling earlier covenants with the church of Central Java – and incurred the wrath of Dr Mulder.

Shortly upon receipt of his letter I wrote a reply in which I reviewed his analysis extensively. I stuck to my point of view and conclusions and suggested that we should meet in order to consider carefully the two evidently colliding views on this twenty-year period. Dr Mulder reacted positively. Our talk took place some time later, with two additional participants. One was the late Mr H. Baas, who after 1954 had served the church of Central Java in various functions and from 1967 onwards was responsible for the relations with Central Java at the mission desk in the Netherlands. For my part, I had asked Revd W. Dijckmeester, pastor of the Netherlands Reformed congregation of which I am a member, to participate in the discussion. I did so because I felt that our talk would go beyond an 'academic' dispute, beyond a comparison of distinct interpretations of a given period. I felt that something like the 'tone' might well determine the ultimate value of the discussion. I asked Revd Dijckmeester to keep an eye on my soul – though I was not really sure what I meant by that.

We met for a number of hours. Each of us felt that something important was at stake, and that our engagement indeed went beyond academic debating. Each of us had formed our diverse images of the mission in the period 1942–1975 in the course of years of involvement. However disparate our views, all of us were profoundly sympathetic to mission work.

In the course of our talk we exchanged many arguments, some of them right down to the finer points. Many elements in the history of the relation between the two churches, events of long ago and more recent ones, were reviewed. The discussion ended on a somewhat surprising note because two things had become clear:

(a) Our difference, i.e. our choices for a specific picture of the period 1942–1975 in the relations between the two churches, had not been bridged. Although much had been clarified, it remained that our 'inductive' approach – continually adding more data – did not yield an integrated image acceptable to each. On the contrary, we interpreted a number of events quite differently.

(b) On the other hand, our talk led to a new 'appreciation'. Evidently, we had struck the right 'tone'. It almost seemed as if our disagreement had taken on new significance. We were aware that this was more than an academic battle for a 'true' story. Both of us were thoroughly familiar with the topic, and threw all we had into the 'fight'. Nevertheless, we did not arrive at a consensus regarding 'the' reality. It appeared that we had reached a certain boundary, to be respected by each. Debate beyond this limit would not yield more insight and even seemed undesirable. In a sense, the legitimacy of the mutually contrasting views seemed strengthened in the course of the discussion. Although the boundary between the two reconstructions of the past remained visible, the breach between them had become less important.

It may be that the way the 'battle between the two stories' was conducted rather than the familiarity with many details, possessed a significance of its own. Evidently, the 'cognitive' difference, the conflict between two views on the relation between two churches, had been relativized. Did this mean that in the course of the debate a space beyond the facts had been accepted, a shared point of moral, political or religious orientation? If so, had this 'beyond' set a new standard for the 'facts' and the debate, and conferred a new meaning on the two stories? What might this new meaning or significance be? Is there a continuity here, such that a new path opens up towards more reliable knowledge and greater maturity of judgement?

ACADEMIC SELF-CRITIQUE IS NOT A GOAL IN ITSELF

Time was that questions regarding the enhancement of understanding via the expansion of knowledge, if indeed it occurred to anyone to ask them, would be answered with unhesitating affirmation. Of course, the 'growth' of the body of scientific knowledge amassed by academic anthropologists is an invaluable aid in understanding what people in other cultures actually feel, value, do and say. Scientific knowledge is the means to inform and improve practice in the broad domains of morality and politics. Science will help us build a better world. The converse came to be assumed as equally self-evident: somehow, political and moral practice are the dynamic agents that offer a perspective, give direction to research and enable scientists to ask relevant questions. Were not the founding fathers of anthropology and developmental sociology, Durkheim, Weber and Marx, each in their own way pristine examples of the bond and interaction of theory and practice?

For the past twenty-five years, however, philosophers at least are not so sure. American philosopher Richard Rorty exposed the poverty of the humanities shortly before the 1980s (*Philosophy and the Mirror of Nature*, 1980) and he continues to experience the 'crisis' to this day: 'The attempt to find laws of history or essences of culture . . . as an aid to understanding ourselves, others and the options we present to one another – has been notoriously unfruitful' (Rorty 1992). The offensive launched by post-modernism shook the foundations of the social sciences, where the organic metaphor of the 'growing body of knowledge' to designate the continued proliferation of scholarly studies was replaced by concepts such as 'genre' and 'narrative'.

The shock reverberated in anthropology and the sociology of development as well. The emergence of reflexive or critical anthropology is a case in point. Reflexive anthropology insists that the study of other cultures is indelibly stamped by our own Western cultural backgrounds, power struggles and preoccupations (Fabian 1983; Parkin 1982).

In the Netherlands, J. Fabian (1983) and some colleagues at the University of Amsterdam have been occupied with rethinking the reliability claim of anthropological knowledge. At one point Fabian asks to what extent and in what way the object of anthropology is construed by anthropologists themselves. It may well be that we are studying something which is part of ourselves. Is it not the case that in our research we continually run into ourselves? Should we not say that the anthropological autobiography conditions the biographies of other cultures? And does this not render knowledge of other cultures basically uncertain and unreliable? Our own 'biographies' cannot be separated from the outcome of scientific analyses; obviously, studies of other cultures are no 'objective' representations, since the researcher is part and parcel of his/her research. Geertz's widely quoted statement that in anthropological research 'anything goes' mirrors the break with earlier empiricist assumptions.

Baudrillard (1990), too, describes the present condition of the social sciences and modern society rather bleakly. We find ourselves, he says, in a situation in which the proliferation of facts, data and general knowledge not only fails to add meaning but erodes it; knowledge increases like a malignant tumour – we are faced with a cultural 'metastasis' in which 'more' may even become lethal. Words and concepts that used to have meaning have lost their substance for both the speaker and the listeners.

Investigating the process of the production of knowledge within its own branch (Crick 1982; Parkin 1982), reflexive anthropology finds that this production – this industrious metaphor enjoyed sudden and ubiquitous popularity during the 1980s – proves susceptible to external political conditioning, fashions, prejudices, susceptible also to the internal power struggle for funds and reputations and to attempts by winners to edge out the losers in this battle.

P. Bourdieu (1993) described scientific 'progress' as the outcome of 'battles' between the established and the outsiders, between the orthodox and the heterodox, quite similar to other 'battlegrounds' in society, such as the world of art, politics, schools, etc. The image of the absent-minded professor who seeks to investigate and understand the world from some sort of 'Archimedian point' (Descartes), an excentric (and eccentric), theoretically founded position, is replaced with the picture of a successful and hence 'orthodox' scientist whom Bourdieu characterizes as a fighter, a manipulator or manager, who takes his stand right in the (still scientific) world. In this way the claim of reliable scientific knowledge seems little more than a thinly disguised lie, a public-relations act intended to nurture the faith in science still clung to by an ignorant non-academic audience. Bourdieu links the reliability claim with the outcome of an internal battle. A good scientist is a successful manager who knows how to secure the profits.

Actually, the suggestion that to fool the public outside the halls of science is useful for the business of science is an older invention. J. Goudsblom (1971) made this recommendation in a different context. His motivation was unlike that of Bourdieu's 'orthodox' scientists. Goudsblom held to the possibility of reliable scientific knowledge. What he denied was that this knowledge was useful. Social relevance was an illusion. He added that social scientists had better keep this insight to themselves, since they might put continued social support of their work at risk. Perhaps, however, we should understand his view on the social utility of science primarily as an attempt to resist the increasingly radicalizing political and revolutionary philosophies of science current at the time.

Successively, then, the attack on the social sciences progressed. Their social utility was politicized or simply denied, the latter probably to retain a bit of space for scientific activities. The next attack was directed against the reliability of scientific statements as such. It seems to me that this move is needlessly self-destructive when it results in giving up the attempt to offer statements which have at least some reliability. A recent dissertation is illustrative of this danger. One of Fabian's students, Robert Pool (1989) drew a prima facie logical conclusion from the insights gained by reflexive anthropology. He relinquished the old objective of science, i.e. the increase of reliable knowledge, when he began his thesis research. The study witnesses to this. It offers a chronological report of the progression of his fieldwork on (perceptions of) diseases in Cameroun. His research no longer offers results. Pool cast his thesis in the mould of a series of successive dialogues between the researcher and various respondents. He rejects the idea that these interviews can be used as a basis for propositions which are abstracted from their context. His respondents cannot be regarded as 'informants' of a cultural context beyond the 'research encounters'. A coherent picture of 'their' perceptions and actions regarding a number of diseases is impossible on principle, he maintains.

The dissertation is based on the conviction that it makes more sense to argue why as researcher you give up the search for objective knowledge than it is to keep trying. He writes:

> I do not assume that there is a 'system of beliefs', or 'culture', somewhere out there in Cameroun, in relation to which my ethnography is, or should be, a mirror image representation. What I present is fiction (in the sense of fictio, something made).
>
> (Pool 1989: 24)

Pool's error is that he separates his own radical-reflexive insights from the context in which they arose. He applies them as a general, independent and de-contextualized perspective on the social sciences.

In fact, Pool fails to apply reflexive anthropology to itself and so commits the error for which he chides others. He ascribes a general value to reflexive insights. But the important contribution of reflexive anthropology was its engagement in a critical debate with an overly self-assured scientific world. Fabian and others provided a counterpoint to this unreflected self-assurance. The pretention that sociology of development and anthropology would 'just' yield reliable knowledge concerning the Third World or other cultures expressed unwarranted triumphalism. The value of reflexive anthropology, therefore, was that it rendered the hegemonic pretensions of these disciplines questionable. A forceful counterpoint to this attitude of the 1970s was well taken.

This does not mean, however, that we must consequently abandon the effort to gain reliable knowledge. It is important to be aware of the fact that the object of investigation and the investigator are linked, and that the reputation of the 'producers' of scientific knowledge is exposed to internal and external political and economic conditioning; certainly, exposed to internal power struggles and manipulation as well. But all of this need not mean that the effort to gain 'objective' knowledge has become irrelevant. At least, the conviction that this effort is of great importance provided the impetus for the intensive exchange of insights recounted in the section above. There was a heated debate about the relevant 'facts'. Years of homework preceded the debate. The good old positivist and pre-positivist belief that there is a true story was never given up, even when the efforts to tell it in an acceptable way were failing at the time. To be sure, moments like that are not plentiful, certainly not within the university. I come back to this below.

THE SEARCH FOR POINTS OF REFERENCE: BEYOND RELATIVISM

The central question in this essay is whether the practical and the scientific knowledge we generate are incommensurable. Is mutual understanding possible, is it possible to build bridges between the distinct domains of practice – scientific or otherwise – and the specific contexts in which these universes of discourse are meaningful? The question can be specified in various ways. One such specification is the dilemma between universalism and relativism. Here the question is whether cross-cultural understanding is possible.

But the problem of the incommensurability of knowledge arises in other contexts as well. It clearly did in the discussion referred to above. Our cultural background was the same, both of us were relatively well informed and earnestly sought to solve our difference; nevertheless, in our analysis at least we did not 'reach' a consensus. Evidently, incommensurability can occur even among people who have much in common.

(a) A first way out? Cognition differences are not the issue; Epstein and Wallace

A noteworthy work was recently published by A.L. Epstein, emeritus professor of anthropology at Sussex. This work, *In the Midst of Life: Affect and Ideation in the World of the Tolai*, is noteworthy because in it Epstein distances himself from his own Manchester School tradition – a tradition featuring a no-nonsense positivism focused on analysis of power constellations and of political and economic change. For a number of years Epstein had exchanged his preoccupation with the usual anthropological themes for analysis of psychological and psycho-analytic issues. But his most recent study brings these experiences to bear on anthropology, a move which leads to a profound criticism of the traditional anthropological approach to culture and cultural differences.

Epstein's basic theme is that the anthropological study of culture has consistently given far too much weight to cognitive dimensions. Concepts and ideas such as worldviews, conceptual representations, cognitions and the like refer primarily to the human being as perceiving, thinking and constructing. This imagery was refined further by ascribing a specific rationality to these cognitive processes: the rationality of architects or engineers 'designing' and 'constructing' reality; the rationality of 'inventors' or 'managers' who 'invent' or 'produce' meaning; the rationality of a fighter in the battle of images or of a bargainer seeking a collective agreement on meanings, etc. In this way every culture could be viewed as standing apart from all other cultures; each a unique construction bearing the stamp of those who fashioned it; each a singular result of bargaining over meanings which in turn were seen as determined by power balances and imbalances among parties. Or: in a sense, the house 'is' the architect, etc. Comparative study of cultures, then, is by definition a doubtful undertaking.

Over against this, Epstein assumes a bond between cognitions and affects. Following the lines of argumentation of some ethnopsychiatrists – especially Tomkins – he argues that cognitions are conditioned by affects. Each affect influences the nature of the cognitions, gives rise to a cognitive field which includes certain cognitions and excludes others. A reverse process occurs as well: these cognitions in turn colour the feelings in which the cognitive field is rooted. Anger, fear, amazement, love, etc. all lead to distinct perceptions of a single environment, context, situation and so on. But those environments differ for every person and for every group. Accordingly, people's perceptions vary widely. Cultural differences, therefore, are normal, everyday phenomena.

But people have the same sorts of feelings. They can recognize them in others, by their facial expressions, by their bodily movements and posture. It is absolutely untrue, says Epstein, that cultures are *completely* different and that comprehension is impossible on account of the differences. To be sure, the variation is enormous. But there is no thoroughgoing incommensurability. On the contrary, there is 'a theoretical expectation of cross-cultural variability'. The knowledge and the experiences of human beings remain recognizable beyond the boundaries of this or that culture because the basic feelings of people are similar in kind. This is why in principle the problem of 'translation' can be solved.

The dilemma between universalism and relativism, Epstein continues, is unauthentic. It arose in an anthropological tradition which one-sidedly emphasized the knowing, designing, cognitive human being. Anthropology allowed itself to be misled: the architects and the bargainers and the fighters were denuded of their emotionality. But just these affects are the shared basis embracing the variety. Cognitive differences were given far too much weight and cut off from their emotive substrate which all people share and hence recognize in their fellows.

Cultural differences arise because the environments in which affects take form are dissimilar. This does not, however, mean that cultures are incommensurable or that understanding across their boundaries is impossible. Affects are commensurable and recognizable; hence understanding is possible: 'Similarity and difference are simply two faces of the same coin' (Epstein 1992: 19).

If this Epsteinian conclusion is combined with an interesting assertion by anthropologist Anthony Wallace (1965), it may well be possible to overcome the dilemma posed by relativism and universalism. Cognitive differences, he says, are inherent to all communication. What he adds, however, is that without these cognitive differences communication would be impossible:

> Indeed, we now suggest that human societies may characteristically *require* the non-sharing of certain cognitive maps among participants in a variety of institutional arrangements. Many a social sub-system simply will not 'work' if all the participants share common knowledge of the system.
>
> (Wallace 1965: 39–40)

For Wallace, differences – individual motives and cognitions – are a necessary condition for human society. Society is inconceivable without acknowledging the paradoxical coherence of misunderstanding and concord. The differences render it continually necessary and desirable for people to engage in – as Wallace calls them – 'contractual relationships'. Shared understanding is a temporary achievement only. After some time it will once again engender a process of misunderstanding and disintegration.

(b) A second way out? Answerable science

The main elevators are to the left as you enter the main building of the Free University, Amsterdam. You won't overlook that building: it towers high above the campus. Stepping into the elevator, though, you may well overlook a modest sign, a small marker placed next to the large number 3 on the neon-lit panel indicating the floor levels. It seems as if the person who had it installed there was unaware of its potential significance and did so without much hope. Next to the number 3 we read: Agora Halls.

Could this minuscule plaquette be a summons to academics to direct their steps to the city's market place? In Greek antiquity the agora was where citizens met to discuss matters of public interest. No political deals were made there: the business of politics was conducted elsewhere. Rather, a leisurely walk across the square made it possible to engage in unhurried discussion and free debate, intent on the clarification of issues and improvement of insight. As such, the agora was one of the most important public institutions of the Greek city-state. Merchants, politicians, philosophers and other citizens mingled together; no one cornered the market.

Implicitly, Wallace and Epstein point in the direction taken by recent studies which invite scientists to leave their own mansions and hovels and to walk about the agora. British philosopher of culture George Steiner holds that unless scientists do so they are fated to suffocate in their airtight houses. A similar call was sounded by participants in a recently published debate (Boomkens 1992) on Rorty's *Contingency, irony and solidarity* (1989).

Both Steiner's book and the authors participating in the Rorty debate start out from the same premise: the claim that scientific theories in one way or another contain references to reality has proved invalid. Attacks against the idea of reliability, and against scientific knowledge pretending to mirror reality, have been rather effective. Neither book contests this state of affairs.

Still, they do not acquiesce either. Unlike certain reflexive anthropologists, these authors do not linger on the battlefield, savouring and reliving the victory. Instead, they turn all of their attention and acumen to the question: Given that its 'modern' foundation has crumbled, how should science proceed? Which path should be taken to restore confidence in the value and reliability of scientific activity?

The ways in which these authors move towards an answer have a common feature: science should re-align itself in its relations with the world of politics (in the broad sense of the word). Or, to stick with the image of the Greek city, science has to frequent the agora again and engage in sustained, open and earnest discussion concerning matters of public interest. If the idea of reliable knowledge no longer refers to a special relationship between scientific theories and 'the' reality, and if, consequently, science can no longer claim reliability on this basis, then 'reliability' must take on a new, political dimension. Scientists have to regain the trust of others in the city. 'Reliable' then means that these others find it worth their while to discuss the results of scientific homework, just as the scientists must participate in discussions touching the polis at large: politics, religion, trade, etc.

Ankersmit's essay (1992) instructively discusses the consequences drawn by Rorty. Commenting on Rorty's treatise of solidarity (1989, 1992), Ankersmit notes that for Rorty this is an a-political concept, since it is formulated in general terms and aimed indiscriminately at every single individual. Rorty's seemingly political conclusion is no more than a sigh of resignation, he states. Are the perceptions, the feelings and the interests of all people identical, then? Are there no differences and contradictions between them? Ankersmit holds that, paradoxically, Rorty remains beguiled by the mirror reflection of the very epistemology he rejects. He merely substitutes one universal for another. Because he rejects the possibility of valid scientific knowledge, Rorty can no longer muster the courage to present a political analysis of the modern world. It wouldn't be valid anyway, would it? But this is why, Ankersmit says, Rorty reveals 'a complete lack of interest . . . in current politics' (Ankersmit 1992: 72) and dares not ask the question 'Why?'

For his part, Ankersmit (1992: 75) disagrees and holds that we certainly should resolve to engage in political analysis. Science should be integrated into the polis, linked with politics, in order to safeguard the openness of public debate and scientific discussion in mutual confrontation, literally responsible and conducted with dignity. The alternative would be that specific interests automatically prevail over the common good, both in science and in politics.

Steiner's (1989) reflections, while following a somewhat different line of thought, turn on the same point of criticism. After many years of post-modernism, scientists seem to retreat to the private sphere and, assuming an attitude of supercilious irony, pretend to remain untouched by the world around them. The conclusion drawn by Steiner is similar to those of Ankersmit (1992: 67) and Stephen Toulmin (1990: 25).

Steiner finds it fatal. He fulminates against the inclination of scientists to retreat to the comfortable and non-committal position of a commentator. He does not hesitate to speak of the *poverty* of the university. This sorry state of science, he writes, is caused by a post-modernism in which basically each point of view is as good as any other. The activity of these commentators is nothing but the 'busy vacancy' or 'high gossip' of those comfortably ensconced back-stage of life. But Steiner adds a profound suggestion as to why there is so little content:

> . . . our current *misère*. It tells of dominance of the secondary and the parasitic. It betrays a radical misconception of the functions of interpretation and of hermeneutics. The latter word is inhabited by the god Hermes . . . messenger between the gods and the living, between the living and the dead, patron also of the resistance of meaning to mortality.
>
> (Steiner 1989: 7)

Note Steiner's point: science is the loser when reflection is disengaged from the political act. In the same context he refers to the concept of the 'speech act' (1989: 18), which joins thought and action. The Hebrew word *daba* suggests a similar insight since it encompasses both thinking and doing, indicating that the two are inseparable.

According to Steiner the wasteland of the post-modern, non-committal and ironic commentaries can be escaped via the restoration of 'immediacy'. He links this concept with the idea of 'polity'; immediacy bridges the gap between interpretation/hermeneutics and the political 'act'. The concept of politics has to be taken in a wide sense here. It means that scientists should expose themselves to responses and reactions from the outside world. A man of letters should do more than write a new commentary on a quatrain of a Shakespearean play which will be read by a handful of colleagues who, of course, react with indignation. That gets us nowhere, Steiner insists. The interpretation has to be 'enacted'. The learned commentator has to go on stage to evoke reaction among the public at large as he enacts his new insight. Science must politicize and so become 'answerable science'. In this way new forms of reliability are created, and universities will perhaps be able to rid themselves of the empty-headed windbags whose pompous commentaries lack meaning and direction.

REVISITING THE CASE: THE VALUE OF CONFLICTING INTERPRETATIONS

The discussion introduced in the opening paragraph ultimately turned on the question as to how the Reformed mission's decision to terminate financial support for the church of Central Java should be interpreted. I mentioned that even an extensive exchange of knowledge regarding background, motives and events did not secure a shared interpretation. It is worthwhile to look into this difference in interpretation more closely. The next question would be what the significance of difference might be. Is it possible to point to a way out, reaching 'beyond' the dead end of facultative interpretations? What then may Bernstein's notion of a beyond be (Bernstein 1983)? In the last paragraph we have suggested two ways in which the notion of similarity and difference may be looked at: linking differing cognitive structures to emotive fields, and the notion of 'agora', public space. Can Epstein's suggestion of the linkage of perceptions and emotions help us further? Should the conflicting interpretations be taken to the market conceived as agora? Must 'scientific' knowledge be taken out of its post-modern encapsulation within the university and be made answerable, in order possibly to gain some sort of significance at all? And, if so, what does that mean? It may be worthwhile to turn back to the case study presented in the beginning of this essay. I shall now try to present a picture of the debate in which not only the contrasting conclusions but also the common ground of our analysis may become apparent. Then I shall look again at the issue of 'similarity' and 'difference' in the interpretations.

(a) Similarity: the role of the intermediaries between mission objective and mission implementation

In our talk we covered a wide range of topics, reviewing many elements in the history of the relation between the two churches against the background of data neither of us felt compelled to contest.

Jointly formulated and implemented by the two churches, the missionary work in Central Java had an unusual structure. After 1950 a Javanese minister and a Dutch missionary bore joint responsibility for the planning and execution of the mission tasks in each of various localities. These regional missionary ministers were the formal representatives of the two churches with rather broad competencies and autonomy *vis-à-vis* their constituency on Java and in the Netherlands respectively. They formulated work plans, concluded arrangements regarding (mostly Dutch) financial support, distributed the funds according to self-set priorities and recruited helpers to carry out the work.

Within a few years one problem facing every policy maker was that Dutch funding became increasingly essential; in a succession of cases the financial contribution from the Javanese side dwindled to virtually none. In other words, a tension arose between, on the one hand, the major objective of the cooperation, i.e. spiritual and material emancipation of the local Javanese churches and, on the other hand, growing dependence of those churches on foreign funds.

Shortly before 1970 the Dutch leadership decided that this situation should end. An internal study had pointed up once again the disproportion in the figures. The working structures on the Dutch side were reorganized. In the place of decentralized cooperation with various regional church communities a central Netherlands agency was created which was to be in touch with the synod of Java. The Javanese missionary pastors were passed by.

Naturally, from the end of the 1950s, whenever the problem of the growing imbalance of the Javanese and Dutch input was discussed, the recurrent and important question was: what caused and perpetuated this process? Basically, the question was answered in two ways. Two kinds of argumentation and analysis evolved, each implying a distinct policy perspective.

The first line of argument blamed the Javanese context for the financial disparity: the Sukarno government's inability to overcome the lasting economic crisis, the abject poverty especially in the rural areas, increasing pressure on the budget of the Javanese church because of its expanding membership particularly in the mid-1960s, etc. There was a ready rapport between these arguments and the theological basis for cooperation: the two churches were jointly responsible for the work, a responsibility given with their biblical calling, the *missio Dei*. It was unthinkable that one would abandon a partner beset by a series of new and seemingly always more serious problems.

The second type of argument located (at least part of) the cause in the cooperation as such. For the policy makers the 'constitution' of poverty rapidly became an increasingly important prerequisite for securing the continuation of the collaboration. The disproportion originated not only in the poverty problem which faced the Javanese churches, but also in the nature of the cooperation and its intrinsic institutional 'interests'. The argument usually posited a connection between two aspects:

1 For the Javanese ministers formulation of the poverty problem had become one of the major strategies in their dealings with the Dutch. Perception of poverty and want, and willingness to alleviate these reinforce one another. In a sense they were interested parties in perpetuating perceptions of deprivation, regardless of whether the poverty problem was escalating or diminishing.

2 Sturdily undergirded canonically and theologically, the formal statement of the 'partner' relationship permitted the Javanese missionary ministers to gain a monopoly in their dealings with the Dutch. *Vis-à-vis* the church in the Netherlands they were the official spokesmen; for their own churches they represented the Dutch views and managed the funds. It is not difficult to imagine that this evoked resistance and that the Javanese believers were becoming reluctant to support the work. Thus 'poverty' constituted not only a precondition for continued collaboration, it also became the outcome of it.

(b) Different interpretations of the policy change

My analysis focused on the personal tragedy experienced by Probowinoto when financial support ended and the old operational structures were pushed aside. Many others, I should add, underwent a similar fate. Is it appropriate to speak of 'tragedy' here?

As I said, both Dr Mulder and I accepted the facts of the case as set out above. Moreover, both of us tended to see the imbalance in the partnership as inscribed in the nature of the cooperation, following the line of the second argument. In other words, as both of us saw it, for an important part the financial dependence of the local church communities was caused and cuddled by the very attempts to overcome it.

Our difference lay elsewhere. In my article I had tried to answer the question as to who was responsible for the *origin* of this form of cooperation. Referring to events occurring in 1947–1948, I had located the cause squarely on the Dutch side. Initially, Probowinoto had considered the partner relationship – joint missionary responsibility – unacceptable and had resisted until swayed by a barrage of theological arguments.

This interpretation differed from the two models of argumentation sketched above. The cause should be located, not in the poverty in Indonesia, not in the interests of go-betweens, but in the Dutch view on missions, which permitted the rise of institutional interests among intermediaries and provided them with theological legitimation. In my PhD thesis (1980) I had emphasized the 'interests' of the intermediaries and the widening distance between them and their constituency. I had described this process in some detail (Quarles van Ufford 1980, chs 5, 6 and 7). At that time, then, I implicitly supported the idea of severing those specific ties. My article on Probowinoto, which introduced the third argument, was an attempt to identify a cause rather than to lay an implicit blame. While the second argument attributed at least part of the problem to the 'doings' and 'interests' of the Javanese policy makers, in my essay on Probowinoto I had stated that the Dutch mission had been responsible for 'pushing' the institutional arrangement upon the Javanese in the first place.

For Dr Mulder, however, it would in the very nature of the case be very hard to share my view. How could I support unilateral severance of the old ties and simultaneously hold the Dutch responsible for the origin of the problem? Mulder had been co-responsible for implementing the new policy, and had to overcome strong opposition along the way. Suppose that he, responsible for policy implementation, had shared my view: would the result not have been that he would introduce notions that tended to sabotage that very same policy? My analysis was utterly unfruitful. Moreover, he said, I had passed over too lightly earlier attempts within the existing organizational arrangements to steer another course. As early as a decade prior to the severance ways were sought to achieve some other form of cooperation. These efforts had failed. In short – but this is a conclusion of mine – the practice of policy implementation and the need to solve the problem placed limits on the search for the problem's cause.

I had been in a different position. In my analysis I was able to question the missionary vision and the resultant policy of the Reformed churches in the Netherlands simply because I was not responsible for them. I had no part in the implementation. Mine was the luxury of being an observer.

(c) Shifting emotions: sympathies and the notion of contingency

My research in the church of Central Java began in the early 1970s. Since then I have intermittently spent lengthy periods on fieldwork, and come to know quite well a number of the major actors there. In the course of my studies my feelings and perceptions regarding the problem of bilateral ecclesiastical cooperation underwent rather incisive change. Initially, I was sympathetic to a number of local pastors who were resisting the powerful regional church leaders, i.e. the intermediary missionary ministers. These pastors received me with hospitality and openness, and the growing friendship may well have contributed to my inclination to lay 'the' problem at the doorstep of the intermediaries. It certainly accorded well with my fascination with the 'local' level. Anthropologists have a well-established tradition to 'build their houses' in a 'local' domain. The struggle and perceptions of these friends of mine could thus become important to me. Moreover, feelings like these were readily legitimized 'scientifically': at the time the literature on patronage provided me with a tailor-made 'scientific' perspective and legitimation for my views.

My broader research objective, however, was to chart the course of the policy process in the long chain of relationships between the Netherlands and Central Java. My research, therefore, implied information-gathering on a variety of organizational levels. Hence, I frequently visited and lodged with the regionally 'powerful' as well, shared their meals and, in spite of my initial local 'sympathies', I gradually became conscious of the fact that more was at issue than I could gather via local respondent-friends. To be sure, the regional functionaries played the power game, adeptly moving the pieces on the chessboard of policy. But I noted with growing clarity that they, the 'powerful', in turn were but pawns moved by other players either in their own Javanese context or in the Netherlands. My initial sympathy with the local pastors who were at odds with their superiors yielded a somewhat one-sided picture. In a sense everyone, from high to low, was essentially vulnerable and powerless because intractable environments and uncontrollable networks had their impact on the work and perceptions of each.

Accordingly, the point of view shifted. The notion of a struggle for power, with a variety of power sources and weaponry and with corresponding distinctions between winners and losers, gradually lost its conceptual relevance. There were no 'winners'. Perhaps the most important characteristic of the policy game played by all these actors was the impossibility to keep events in check. I became aware of the essential and pervasive *contingency* which clung to the policy process.

Another stint of fieldwork in Central Java during the 1980s greatly strengthened the feeling that essential powerlessness and contingency were thoroughly interwoven with the policy process. A number of regional missionary ministers (the intermediaries) were in total bewilderment as they had been put aside, abandoned by nearly all their former fellow players. Living conditions of those who had no private income were deplorable. One of these 'retired' Javanese missionary ministers showed me the formal documents confirming his appointment to the post and let me touch the seals embossed on them. He showed me official agreements, exchanges of letters and even a series of articles of his in Dutch newspapers – eagerly published by the very friends who had now turned away from him. He was still nonplussed as to how these things could come to pass. Although he was aware that certain people had made certain moves, he could not identify a cause or lay a blame. It just happened.

His plight prompted me to plead his cause to some in his own environment. I tried to explain to a number of his 'opponents' – the local pastors who had befriended me a decade earlier – how I saw the history of the conflict. I pictured their 'opponent' as a man who may have had his faults, but also as a man who carried out a task assigned and entrusted to him, a task to which he had dedicated his working life.

What happened to my privileged position as cultural anthropologist, as non-responsible onlooker? I was in a quandary, my sympathies a medley. Did it make sense to speak of 'responsibilities'? What was the point of searching out 'the' ultimate cause of the problems? Cause and effect, guilt and responsibility: the context rendered them more and more elusive – and perhaps less relevant.

It is not inconceivable, therefore, that my analysis of the 'tragic' dimension in the life of Probowinoto was a way of escaping my confusion. Surely, somebody was responsible? Or, at least, a chain of causes and effects commences somewhere, does it not? Did I perhaps write the paper because so far no-one had pointed an accusing finger at the Dutch, especially their role in an earlier period, when with a barrage of theological arguments, they had pushed their ecclesiastical self-perceptions upon Probowinoto? This might well be the case.

And, if so, a respectable academic legitimization, referring to the fact that I had been engaged in follow-up fieldwork and was by now 'well informed', would amount to a mere sleight of hand. We all know the standard phrase: 'Further study has now demonstrated that . . . '. But what actually happened was this: the outcome of my follow-up research is now that a conceptually tractable chain of causes and effects blurred into a contingent succession of events.

It is, of course, entirely possible that once again I committed a comparable 'error' – clarity at the cost of truth – in my Probowinoto article of 1987, when I constructed a new 'starting point' for understanding successive events. It may well have been a new effort to preclude the conclusion of contingency. This judgement, however, must be left to others. I will touch again on this point in the concluding section.

(d) Debate and agora

The call sounded by Steiner and Ankersmit to engage in answerable science derives its value for an important part from the insight that the quality of scientific knowledge erodes if the walls of the house of science become prison walls. The house becomes a prison also if pride keeps us there. The inevitable result is trouble: prison revolts, sometimes even casualties. Post-modernism is a case in point because it induces people to give up the search for reliable knowledge.

The open space in the heart of town is vitally important for all. We should restore the idea of the market to its old Greek significance and win it back from the merchants who have appropriated it – 'goods' are not always up for sale.

But the call should be sounded loud and clear, for it must be heard above the institutional din. Universities, for example, are subject to various sorts of pressure to close their ranks and to cloak their vulnerability. The old handbooks are wrong when they tell us that in the forum of colleagues alone flourishes 'true' science. Moreover, what holds for institutionalized learning is equally true for all sorts of modern organizations. Every respectable institution, including a church denomination, will take its decisions only after 'all advantages and disadvantages were considered extensively and weighed with care'. An astounding and still proliferating number of mantras is currently in use to legitimize the unique value of one's own forum and the importance of warding off the outside world. There is money in thinking up new mantras. We know very well, though, that mantras are dissemblers. The call to go to the market may involve risk and danger, but remains of vital importance.

Sometimes the call is heeded even now. And when it is, the market proves an important place. This was certainly my experience when I was told that my scientific analysis left something to be desired and that a number of things should be put right. I did not concur, but having walked about the market in earnest conversation I came to understand the value of listening closely. It was not that I would have to capitulate, nor did I do so. But the path to new queries and new reflection was repaved. I learned, for example, that each of us initially (mis-)took our own story for 'the' history of the relation between the two churches. After all, we dealt with something we considered important, to which we had dedicated years of our life. It is probable that this emotion evoked in us an obdurate, 'positivistic' attitude, and that we sought to convince each other by a barrage of facts and arguments. Perhaps, too, the fact that different feelings played a part in our stories precluded agreement. While I had stayed at the homes of my local friends as well as of their bosses over a long period of time, I had come to sympathize with the vulnerabilities of each, looking for 'first causes' further in the past. For Dr Mulder the same must have been at stake. His life-world came to encompass, moreover, the domain of missionary policy-making with its own rationales and limitations to analysis. He had to take decisions, that is, to achieve clarity and engage in action. He would in this capacity have to stick to his story of the past for some time. He was required to defend his views legitimately and convincingly to his constituency, and certainly for himself. Accepting my views and analysis would only hamper his capacity to 'do' something. I did not share his responsibilities. And so, perhaps, the most significant part of the debate was its ending. We both stopped trying to convince the other of 'the' truth of our own analysis. We both stuck to our insights, yet in some way or another I had begun to realize that each analysis of the past was basically contingent and informed by different domains (the political and the academic). The agora is a public place and other citizens were listening in.

CONCLUDING REMARKS

The disagreement between Dr Mulder and me is but one case pointing up the ubiquitous tension, perhaps even contradiction, between the dynamics of gathering knowledge and the process of judgement. The more that is known about some topic or issue, the harder it becomes to formulate reliable judgements. On the other hand, one's research is usually guided by a 'hunch' or a feeling. There is a judgement to begin with, a ready-made design for a coherent picture which for some time remains implicit, personal and largely unreflected. Accordingly, scientific activity is an essentially contradictory business. This was exactly how I experienced it when over many years I kept returning for periods of fieldwork in the same locality.

The problem of the incommensurability of scientific and practical knowledge could arise because this contradiction was denied or not recognized. Conventional 'modern' science is predicated on the myth that 'cognitive knowledge' as such is possible and that to achieve reliability, perhaps redefined as intersubjectivity, science must take the path of an abstraction, i.e. to fit the data into a theory or a model. This fiction evoked its mirror reflection in post-modernism which rejected the older definition of reliability and concluded that every attempt to gain scientific reliability is in pursuit of nothing but illusion.

The present volume explores possibilities to escape the choice between relativism and essentialism. A number of suggested answers were introduced, whereby the concept of reliability is defined in a variety of related ways. A worthwhile question is whether these answers, in spite of their evident differences, have some feature in common. As I see it, the common denominator among them is that they consciously and consistently introduce *uncertainties*. Each of the answers points to the *contingency* of cognitive knowledge. The rationality of the activity of critical science and critical thinking is limited. This limitation has to be made visible. And this, in turn, happens whenever critical scientific rationality is openly exposed to the unpredictable influences of other domains of human existence. This does not detract from the value of critical rationality but actually enhances its value.

David Wong (1989) argues that the task of science is not only to overcome the limitations and contingencies of existence, but also to give *expression* to them. Commenting on some statements by Charles Taylor, he writes: 'We must grasp an older conception of rationality that makes no distinction between understanding the world and coming into attunement with it' (Wong 1989: 143). What does it mean to say that 'attunement' counts as a mark of quality of scientific activity? It means, first of all, that the fiction of 'success assured' if only reflection and critical research are allowed to pursue their own objectives in isolation should be abandoned. Uncertainties and contingencies have to be expressed.

Epstein spoke of linkages between emotions and cognitions. This means not only that the anthropologist has to place the individuals or groups studied in a broader context than is hitherto customary. It further implies, reflectively, that the researcher should be more than an impersonal magnifying glass and a laptop. The inevitable result is that fieldwork will pose new challenges: there is a very real tension between observation and participation.

This does not mean that I am advocating 'action research' on the argument that this would be the most suitable way to expose the researcher as actor. No. Once again I want to refer to the metaphor of the market place. At the market we experience that a vast gulf separates commentary, explanation and research from action, responsibility and decision-making, and simultaneously understand that we are able to take steps to close the gap. It is at the market that we experience the unpredictable and thrilling event which Steiner calls 'immediacy', where the confrontation between commentary and act is filled with new tension. The agora is important because it refers to the unpredictability of the encounter, the communication and the reaction. This unpredictability opens the possibility that the contingencies of everyone's activity, scientific and otherwise, be made visible. This is why the agora is the place for attunement. We have to walk to it from time to time in order to get some fresh air.

Many current authors stress openness towards contingency. Some in addition refer to an aspect or dimension which, as I see it, embraces all other aspects: faith. Commenting on our post-modern times, van Harskamp (1990) deals explicitly with the question of the meaning of faith. He concludes that faith is essential, because it grants us the courage to confront uncertainties and contingencies and in so doing to overcome the emptiness of our fragmented daily life. I readily agree with him. At the end of the discussion with Dr Mulder we both may have to come to realize that our stories were expressive of our best possible understanding. I still believe that my 'story' is true and reliable. Yet similarity and difference of the two stories are indeed two sides of the same coin. We stopped the debate and let it be. When at the end we left the market place it had become clear to me that, paradoxically, by silently acknowledging the contingency of my own story, its value had only increased.

Faith in God's grace, too, may thus be a tangible, everyday event relevant for understanding and actions in the domains in which we do our work. If so, the agora may be pictured as a churchyard. At the beginning of his book Steiner says something that comes down to the same thing:

> This essay . . . proposes that any coherent understanding of what language is and how language performs, that any coherent account of the capacity of human speech to communicate meaning and feeling is, in the final analysis, underwritten by the assumption of God's presence.
>
> (Steiner 1989: 3)

Knowledge at its most reliable arises when silently we open ourselves and acknowledge our contingencies, allowing for the presence of God. I would like to end with a reference to Psalm 78, a psalm whose theme is history. The story tells us about the successive generations, the relation between parents and children. The psalmist enjoins parents to recount the great works of Jaweh to their children in a way which allows for a space for understanding which is not their doing and thus makes a difference.

He established a testimony in Jacob,
and appointed a law in Israel,
which he commanded our fathers
to teach to their children;
that the next generation might know them,
the children yet unborn,
and arise and tell them to their children,
so that they should set their hope in God,
and not forget the works of God,
but keep his commandments;
and that they should not be like their fathers,
a stubborn and rebellious generation,
a generation whose heart was not steadfast,
whose spirit was not faithful to God.

The children should hear about the deeds of the Lord, *so that* [!] they will hope in God and *not* be like their parents.

REFERENCES

Ankersmit, F. (1992) 'De grondslagenvijandige politieke filosofie van Richard Rorty' in R. Boomkens (ed.) *De asceet, de tolk en de verteller*, Amsterdam: Krisis Onderzoek, 58–76.

Baudrillard, J. (1990) *La Transparance du Mal: Essais sur les Phénomènes Extrêmes*, Paris: Editions Galilee.

Bernstein, R. (1983) *Beyond objectivism and relativism: Science, hermeneutics and praxis*, Philadelphia: University of Pennsylvania Press.

Boomkens, R. (ed.) (1992) *De asceet, de tolk en de verteller: Richard Rorty en het denken van het Westen*, Amsterdam: Krisisonderzoek.

Bourdieu, P. (1993) *Sociology in Question*, London: Sage Publications.

Crick, M. (1982) 'Anthropological field research, meaning creation and knowledge construction' in D. Parkin (ed.) *Semantic anthropology*, London: Academic Press, 15–39.

Epstein, A. L. (1992) *In the midst of life: Affect and ideation in the world of the Tolai*, Berkeley: University of California Press.

Fabian, J. (1983) *Time and the other: How anthropology makes its object*, New York: Columbia University Press.

Goudsblom, J. (1971) *Balans van de sociologie*, Utrecht: Aula.

Parkin, D. (ed.) (1982) *Semantic anthropology*, London: Academic Press.

Pool, R. (1989) *There must have been something; Interpretations of illness and misfortune in a Cameroon village*, Amsterdam: University of Amsterdam.

Quarles van Ufford, P. (1980) *Grenzen van internationale hulpverlening*, Assen: Van Gorcum.

—— (1987) 'Probowinoto: An exemplary Indonesian Christian' in Nico L. Kana and N. Daldjoeni (eds) *Ikrar dan Ikthiar dalam hidup pendeta Basoeki Probowinoto*, Jakarta: BPK Gunung Mulia, 165–82.

Rorty, R. (1980) *Philosophy and the mirror of nature*, Princeton: Princeton University Press.

—— (1989) *Contingency, irony and solidarity*, Cambridge: Cambridge University Press.

—— (1992) 'Heidegger, Kundera en Dickens: de rol van filosofie en literatuur bij het vergelijken van culturen', in R. Boomkens (ed.) *De asceet, de tolk en de verteller*, Amsterdam: Krisis Onderzoek, 19–39.

Steiner, G. (1989) *Real presences: Is there anything in what we say?*, London: Faber and Faber.

Toulmin, S. (1990) *Kosmopolis: De verborgen agenda van de moderne tijd*, Kampen: Kok Agora.

Van Harskamp, A. (1990) 'Geloven zonder küng zekerheid? Aantekeningen over de postmoderne tijd en het geloof' in H. Kung et al., *Godsdienst op een keerpunt*, Kampen: Kok, 85–134.

Wallace, A. F. C. (1965) *Culture and personality*, New York: Random House.

Wong, D. B. (1989) 'Three kinds of incommensurability' in M. Krausz (ed.) *Relativism: Interpretation and confrontation*, Notre Dame: Notre Dame University Press, 140–59.

3

METHODOLOGICAL LUDISM

Beyond Religionism and Reductionism

André Droogers

Over twenty years ago, as a new anthropologist, using the method of participant observation, I witnessed a boys' initiation ritual in a small Zairean tribal society, the Wagenia of Kisangani (Droogers 1980). This rite of passage had not been held for fourteen years. For five months almost the whole tribe of about 8,000 people was busy staging the initiation. More than 1,300 boys, aged between 5 and 20, were isolated in fourteen camps. The ritual accompanied the boys during a transition in their life. It did so by using symbols in dramatic and social contexts that were part of its various phases.

My training provided not only the method of participant observation – in fact a simulated participation – but also the stereotypical expectation that ritual is a religious phenomenon, and that initiation is a vehicle for the transmission of culture, especially religion. Besides, Africans were supposed to be incurably religious (e.g. Thomas et al. 1969: 5). I soon found out, however, that Wagenia reality was different. Their reflection and behaviour were to correct my academic discourse.

The initiation ritual was mainly secular. It contained only a few religious references, principally to spirits of the dead, as when the boys were painted white, the colour of the spirits, in order not to be harassed by them. Moreover, the Wagenia boys' initiation proved to be a rather boring experience for most of them. Explicit transmission of culture hardly occurred. The main thing the novices learned – but most of them had known before – was wrestling. Besides, a lot of time was invested in training an imitation of a military parade observed in town. In this make-believe parade the older boys played the role of the civil and ecclesiastical authorities. The oldest novice, who acted as the chief of the camp, was given the role of the state president, Mobutu. The smallest boy played the role of the region's archbishop, a man of very small stature.

Though predominantly secular, the ritual was reminiscent in some respects of religion. There were a few secrets that the non-initiated, especially the women, were supposed not to know, but that almost all of them were acquainted with. Yet the women played their role of outsiders, almost as I played my role of insider. Thus, the women were supposed to believe that the boys in the camp stayed day and night unprotected in the open air, except when it started raining. Then a big bird with enormous wings came to the camp to offer the boys shelter from the rain. A bird-like sound was heard from the camp, and the men and the boys chanted and danced to the rhythm of the bird's song. As most of the women knew, this bird was not a bird at all, but represented the hut in the camp, built in a U-form, with a 'breast' and 'wings', as of a bird. The sound of a bird was imitated by an instrument made out of two sticks and a big shell. At other stages in the initiation two more 'animals' were enacted by the men, again using musical instruments, always with the suggestion that the women were being led to believe that extraordinary beings manifested themselves. Here too the women played their role, but knew what was being staged.

This was my first experience with an intriguing mixture of profane and seemingly sacred elements. Besides the 'normal' religious element of the belief in spirits of the dead, there was an enacted element that might be called religioid. The men and women played at religion, as the novices did when teaching the smallest boy to act as an archbishop. It was obvious that everything was played, but also that the illusion was maintained in a strict manner, as if it were real. The ludic seemed part of a religious, or at least religioid, atmosphere. Of course, my participant's role was also an illusion, a method of make-believe, though not religious or religioid in nature, although the Wagenia word for white man was the same as that for spirit of the dead.

About ten years later, when doing fieldwork in a Brazilian spiritist healing group, I had another confusing experience that led me to the ludic (Droogers 1991). The group was composed of about thirty people, many of them with an academic training. Its leader, a medical doctor, had developed a specific method of spiritist healing. It was a combination of spiritist, Christian, Afro-Brazilian and medical insights. As was the case in Zaire, some form of enactment seemed to occur, at least to me. But now the playfulness was not a manifest part of the participants' view; it had much more to do with my own academic bias and corresponding presuppositions. In this case, the ludic – though not fully absent from the people's behaviour – was primarily a promising concept in my search for an explanation. Perhaps the experience with the Wagenia influenced me in my way of looking at these spiritists.

The group attributed the affliction of the patient to demonic spirits. One of these spirits was made to manifest himself in a spirit medium. The coordinator of the healing session then started a severe but often also rather humorous and ironic – ludic, I would say – dialogue with the spirit, with the ultimate intention to convert him, often 'in Jesus' name'. The converted spirit would then stop his attacks on the patient and would accept to continue his evolutionary course through a morally progressive series of reincarnations. Normally the spirit would first resist and utter blasphemous statements, but gradually he would give in. Often he was referred to a hospital in the spirit world in order to prepare for reincarnation.

Thus, in a few minutes, a small drama of transition, a rite of passage, was enacted – at least that was my interpretation – in which the cause of the patient's affliction was first made real. Very often the demonic spirit was shown to have sought revenge for acts his victim had committed against him in a former life. This cause was subsequently eliminated through the conversion of the spirit, and sometimes also by a reconciliation with the patient. Like the boys' initiation, the healing process produced a transformation in a symbolic and dramatic way, within a social context, and in a consecutive series of phases. In my view, then as now, metaphors were used as effective resources.

To the participants the spirits were real; here was no question of a useful illusion. On the contrary, in a book the group's leader presented the healing method as a new science (Lacerda de Azevedo 1988). Knowledge was constructed within a socio-political context in which scientific knowledge was supposed to represent the highest standard. As an academic doing research among academics and formally addressed as 'professor', I was constantly challenged by my spiritist friends to position myself and to agree with them. My research was to validate their method. The group's leader wanted me to take the message to Europe and spread it there. However, my participant observation was much more observation than participation. Despite the fact that several members of the group affirmed that I could be a good spirit medium, I remained an outsider. Yet, if I did not accept their discourse about the manifestation of spirits, I would have to look for another explanation for their behaviour, and most of all for their healing successes.

In both fieldwork experiences, I had come with the metropolitan academic discourse I had been trained to use, but both times I was challenged to change my mind. The people I studied taught me to look for other dimensions: in Zaire for religion in playfulness, in Brazil for religion in science. Their behaviour and reflection rendered my type of discourse problematic. The Wagenia proved not to be as religious as I had supposed them to be; the Brazilian spiritist academics were not as secular as I had expected them to be. Supposedly religious Africans were enacting a secular play with some religioid characteristics, whereas supposedly secular Brazilians were in a very serious manner enacting a drama with religious entities, presenting their view as a new erudite science, although I sometimes found them as playful and inventive as the Wagenia.

In both cases, the secular and the religious were intermingled in a fascinating and puzzling manner. Religious and non-religious factors competed for priority in the explanation of the phenomena I had observed. How seriously was religion to be taken? How far was religion something essentially playful? How was religious knowledge being constructed, and how was my academic knowledge of religion constructed? When studying religion and ritual, what was the value of enacted participation as a method? Did informant and researcher have in common the fact that both were players?

THE PROBLEM

Doing social science implies debate. Any debate has its own map of options, often based on dichotomies, like mind/matter, self/other and nature/culture, that have been with us for a long time already. What can I do, as a social scientist, when involved in such a theoretical or interpretative debate? Should the options be accepted as permanent and for ever inevitable? Or is there a way to go beyond the well-known options? If there is a way out, would I be able to follow it without abandoning my own preferences?

The conflict under discussion in this contribution is that between a reductionist and a religionist view of religion. Reductionism has also been called naturalism, emphasizing religion as an aspect of human nature (Preus 1987: ix). Yet, not all naturalists are necessarily reductionists. Since the reductionist method is my main concern, I will use the term reductionism, even though it is not a perfect mirror term of religionism.

Although in the course of time a whole spectrum of varying and nuanced opinions has been developed on both sides (see the next section), the original issue is still basic to the current discussion (Idinopulos and Yonan 1994, for a recent example). The central question under debate is whether religion can adequately and totally be explained by exclusive reference to non-religious facts and factors. The debate is asymmetrical in that the problem is not so much a cause of concern to reductionists as it is to religionists.

Reductionists, mainly but not exclusively social scientists, usually explain religion by referring to psychic and social characteristics of human life. Reductionists will maintain that it is perfectly possible to explain religious behaviour, including believers' opinions about the truth of the sacred, by appealing to non-religious factors, and without reference to a supernatural reality that is supposed to manifest itself. They will not exclude participants' opinions from their data and their explanation of religious behaviour, but they will not regard them as truths about the sacred, as religionists – directly or indirectly – do. From the reductionists' point of view, theirs is an adequate use of informants' views, and consequently there is no problem at all. Therefore they will refer to the religionists' claim that the manifestation of the sacred is an important element in the explanation of religion as a non-debate. They generally do not see the need to refer to a sacred reality and may find the use of the word 'reality' at the least dubious in the case of the supernatural, even though they may accept, as a fact to be explained, that the supernatural is something real and 'natural' to believers. To reductionists the supposed truth of these beliefs in a sacred reality is in itself not an element in their scholarly study of religion, but only the fact that people say it is true. Even if, in a hypothetical case, some day the beliefs in question were shown to be really true, it still remains to be explained why people accept them.

Conversely, in the religionist view, defended mainly but not exclusively by scholars from the phenomenology and history of religions, and not by all of them, an explanation of religion takes into account that the 'other' reality that is the object of religious activity can manifest itself. Religion would not exist without people's experiencing this other reality, and therefore its manifestation should be part of the explanation. The comparative approach excludes the acceptance of the views expressed by one particular religion on this manifestation. Accordingly, less specific notions of the sacred are adopted, implying that specific religions express particular views on this universal sacred. The sacred that manifests itself is supposed to be paralleled by human capacities, such as the production of symbols.

Despite – or perhaps because of – this wide gap between religionists and reductionists, I shall explore a solution that leads beyond the familiar options. I look for it in the notion of the ludic, or playfulness. The hunch that the ludic might show a way out of the problem has been with me for some time now, as may have become clear from the brief autobiographical reference to some of my anthropological fieldwork experiences, just as these same experiences put the relation between religion and science on my agenda. But first of all a more detailed appraisal of the conflict between religionism and reductionism is needed – as it were the map of the available options. Then this appraisal is applied to the cases presented in the introduction. After that the notion of the ludic is discussed. The next section puts the theme within an interdisciplinary framework. In the penultimate section, the lessons of the preceding sections are compared in order to explore the chances of finding a way beyond old repeated options. A conclusion summarizes the argument.

RELIGIONISM AND REDUCTIONISM: THE OPTIONS

It is useful to make an inventory of the options that are at stake in the religionism/reductionism debate. Clarke and Byrne (1993), Guthrie (1993: 8–38), Idinopulos and Yonan (1994), and Segal (1989) are recent sources for such an inventory. The making of an inventory is necessary because of the fact that defenders of one of the two main positions have come to differ among themselves. The debate on religionism and reductionism has accordingly entered a stage in which nuances have come to characterize the positions. Yet the basic watershed is still the same.

The central question can be formulated as a choice between two alternatives: Must religion be explained in terms which refer to a sacred reality that manifests itself (religionism); or should the explanation of religion be exclusively 'humanistic' and limit itself to a psychological and sociological framework, referring to human conditions that are external to religion (reductionism)?

A common distinction is that between methodological theism, agnosticism and atheism: in explaining religion and for methodological purposes the student accepts that a sacred reality exists (methodological theism); abstains from an opinion about this issue (methodological agnosticism); or denies the existence of the sacred (methodological atheism). In scholarly practice the second position has the same effect as the third, but its proponents, in suspending a judgement, intend to show more respect for other people's beliefs.

The adjective 'methodological' suggests that the options are valid in research alone. The scholar may cherish another opinion in private. A reductionist may opt for methodological atheism or agnosticism, while being a theist in private. This is possible precisely because of the fact that to him or her the truth question is not an element in the explanation of religion. Religionists will most probably be religious persons, but this does not exclude far-going variations between their religious convictions. The fact that religions differ in their truth claims implies that religionists must in some way position themselves, either opting for a certain religion, or accepting some basic general view on the sacred that is supposed to manifest itself in all religions. Yet, in the latter case a preference for a certain religion as the best expression of the sacred is still possible. In short, private opinions and scholarly convictions can but need not coincide.

One should be aware that these views did not develop in an ideological vacuum, but were part of an intellectual struggle concerning the right definition of reality. In terms of the sociology of knowledge, the question is in what social and cultural context the construction of an academic discourse takes place. This means that what is normal and natural in our own cultural context should be considered problematic, and even treated as exotic. This applies to religionists as well as reductionists.

Religionists developed their views in the context of expanding Western culture. The history of Western expansion had rehabilitated what were formerly considered barbarous societies as civilizations. It became possible to study the so-called 'world religions' linked to these civilizations, to collect their texts and to document their rituals. Comparisons could be made. Religion in the singular, as a human capacity, came to the fore. Inspired by philosophical phenomenology, methods were developed that should guarantee a scientific quality and a certain correctness of the observations, excluding the Western bias. Many of the new theories were reductionist in nature, but some, inspired by a form of modern liberal Christian theology, maintained the idea of a common manifestation of the sacred behind the diversity of religions. Religionists have had to defend themselves on two fronts, against science, and against Christian theology. The latter conflict was caused by the coexistence of 'Comparative Religion' and Christian theology in the same department. This ungrateful position of 'attack and defence' (Sharpe 1975: 144) seems to have contributed to the formulation of a religionist point of view by such scholars as Söderblom, Otto and Van der Leeuw. Using other sources Eliade arrived at a similar position.

The adoption of a non-religious frame of reference, especially in methodological atheism, is nourished by Enlightenment science's scepticism and the critical question raised by the rise of modernity of why religion should exist at all (Clarke and Byrne 1993: 28, 32, 40). Criticism of religion has often been the main motive to seek for an explanation: how could people believe in an illusion? Behind their objectivity, scholars were taking part in the secularization process, and occupying positions in the competition between religious and scientific world-views. The debate between religionists and reductionists, though different in essence, cannot be isolated from this conflict. It is its hidden agenda. If reductionists qualify it as a non-debate, the – rather arrogant – presupposition is that science has overcome religion and dictates the norms. One of the two parties wants to take the place of the judge.

The reductionist goal of producing a *general* theory of religion as such, understood in the universal singular, necessarily leads to the exclusion of religious explanations, because the latter are supposed to be linked to particular religions (Clarke and Byrne 1993: vii, viii, 28). The most common explanations in this category refer to such non-religious functions as wish fulfilment, the social order, or cognition (Guthrie 1993: 10). Ironically, the reductionist attention given to function has led to a definition of religion in which not the supernatural or the transcendental was the criterion, but the unity of the group or the resolution of ultimate existential questions. As a consequence, what formerly had been called secular, like ideology or even science, came to be viewed as religious.

Though maintaining the basic option, some amendments have been formulated (Clarke and Byrne 1993: 55, 73, 74; Segal 1989: 126–9). Thus, on the religionist side, it has been suggested that the specific forms religions show are only symbolic approximations of a sacred reality that is by definition beyond our knowledge. In this way a general theory can be maintained without embracing a specific religion. Similarly, on the reductionist side some have advocated a symbolic approach, advancing the idea that religious expressions are not what they seem to be, but refer symbolically to another – in this case secular – reality.

Another refinement has occurred with regard to the question of how the opinions of the religion's participants should be appreciated. Straightforward religionism would accept them as true and valid in the explanation of that religion. When, in a less strict form of religionism, religions are understood as expressions of a sacred, unknowable reality, the participants' views are heard for their symbolic referential value. On the reductionist side, if emphasis is put on the mechanistic role of structures, less attention tends to be given to participants' views, especially if some supra-individual structural mechanism is considered responsible for the rise of religion. Yet, the symbolic approach in reductionism will include participants' beliefs and behaviour in its explanation, since these contain information on the symbolic system. Related to this, but for other reasons, an actor-centred approach will in any case consider the believer's religious point of view. Similarly, when it is considered a basic human characteristic that people confer meaning – though not necessarily religious meaning – to reality, participants' views are basic data in research (Segal 1989: 109–35).

EXPERIENCES AND OPTIONS CONFRONTED

The fieldwork experiences related in the first section may be commented on in the light of these central questions. Thus, experiencing the spirits of the dead was a reality that was not subject to discussion to my Wagenia and Brazilian informants. To me it was out of the question that their opinions were part of my data, just as I admitted the vague notion that there might be more between heaven and earth . . . . My personal problem in participant observation was of course whether as a researcher I accepted that my informants were right and that spirits were real, especially as my Brazilian informants did much to try to convince me.

Yet, my scepticism obliged me to look for other explanations, like attributing healing power to metaphors. To complicate things, my scepticism did not mean that I deny the existence of the autonomous reality that religionist authors allude to. As a Christian working in an ecumenical university, holding the chair of the cultural anthropology of religion, and standing in a secular social science tradition, it is my job to make sense of religion. It may cause no surprise that I take the religionism/reductionism debate as my test-case and seek to go beyond the established options.

The ambiguity of my position also implies that, in a rather eclectic way, I see the value of reductionist theories of the three types mentioned by Guthrie (1993: 10), also when dealing with the above-related fieldwork experiences. With regard, first of all, to *wish fulfilment*, anxiety reduction plays a role in both the Wagenia and Brazilian case described above. The Wagenia boys who paint their body with white clay are seeking protection, believing that spirits can be deceived. When they and their fathers dance with the 'big bird', they are at the same time reassuring their mothers and experiencing male security and unity. The Brazilian spiritist healers are seeking relief for their patients by eliminating the spiritual cause of the affliction.

The interpretation of religion that focuses on *social order* can also be applied to the cases just presented. The Wagenia spirits of the dead represent the continuity of society. The initiation ritual reinforces social structural distinctions related to age, gender and kinship. The whole ceremony accompanies the boys' transition from the world of women and children to that of the men. In the case of the Brazilian healing group, their battle against demons is a way of establishing a social order based on charity. Both Wagenia novices and Brazilian spiritists were constructing their identity.

The third group of interpretations, of a more *cognitive* nature, also applies to my fieldwork cases. The Wagenia initiation ritual can be understood as an effective manner of accompanying boys on their way from childhood to manhood, even though the low frequency of the ritual means that the youngest boys are still too young and the oldest already too old to reach this result. Yet, because some of the fundamental organizing principles of their society are active in initiation, all boys become acquainted with them. Even though education in the strict sense hardly takes place, the ritual therefore has educational value. Cognitive aspects are also present in the spiritist practice. They not only present their method as a new science, but also include religious categories, like demonic spirits and Jesus, in what they see as a scientific interpretation of affliction.

It may be clear that even a generous eclectic use of theories of religion does not exhaust the cases described. None of the theories allows for the playfulness present, especially in the Wagenia case, and also, in my view, among the spiritists of the healing group. It seems that in the religious context there is a margin for experiments and creativity. Even experiments with make-believe are possible. The boundary between the possible and the real is vague. All these considerations led me to the idea that the ludic could not only be an underestimated dimension in religion, but could also offer a way out of the dilemma between religionism and reductionism. Epistemological questions (raised at the end of the first section) contributed to that idea.

It may seem a case of flogging a dead horse if I now explore a trail beyond the dichotomy of religionism and reductionism. Yet, scientific paradigms are tenacious and resilient. Usually they are still very much alive outside the discipline in which they have been declared dead for some time. Besides, the amended frames of reference have still not dealt with the challenge of the religious and theological explanations of religion. Methodological theism remains taboo among most social scientists, despite lip-service to postmodernism. The discussion may have become less outspoken within social scientific approaches to religion, but the dialogue with colleagues from comparative religion has hardly started. As will have become clear from this and the first section, I also have a personal interest in exploring new perspectives, since these may help me to clarify my position as a scholar of religion and as a religious scholar.

As I will show, the dimension I add to the debate has relevance for the interdisciplinary study of religion. Its claim goes beyond the current discussion between religionists and reductionists, and it sheds a different light on religion and on the explanation of religion. Before this can be shown, the concept of the ludic must first be discussed.

THE LUDIC

It is almost impossible to give an adequate overview of what has been written on the ludic. The literature on the subject is vast and at the same time extremely diverse and even contradictory. There is an obvious difference whether one refers to games and sports, or to theatre, or to a child's way of playing, or to animals' play, or to power games in political strategy – to mention only a few of the examples authors have taken as their starting-point. In view of my particular interest I have made my own selection and summary from the material that was available. This means that I will ignore some important authors in the field, and give preference to others who may be not so well-known.

A working definition of the ludic, adapted to my purposes, can be formulated as follows: the ludic is *the capacity to deal simultaneously and subjunctively with two or more ways of classifying reality.*

With regard to the term 'subjunctive', I follow Victor Turner who distinguishes between the 'indicative mood', the domain of the 'as is', and 'the subjunctive mood . . . used to express supposition, desire, hypothesis, or possibility', the domain of the 'as if' (Turner 1988: 25, 169).

Simultaneity is the other defining term. Pruyser (1976: 190) attributes to the player a 'double awareness'. Huizinga, who with his 'Homo Ludens' (1952) contributed immensely to our understanding of the ludic, has emphasized the seriousness of play, even though he has been criticized for not sufficiently emphasizing the simultaneity of seriousness and play (Ehrmann 1968: 33; Pannenberg 1984: 323, 324). According to the critics the ludic is not an extra, but part and parcel of human reality. The compartmentalization and pluralism that are characteristic of modern society have made us blind to that characteristic. In Victor Turner's terms: the 'indicative mood' has overcome the 'subjunctive mood' (1988: 101). The ludic has been exiled to its own sphere. Modern society has thereby lost sight of play's real nature. As we will see below, postmodernism has partly recovered this perspective.

Thanks to simultaneity, things can be discriminated and yet equated, just as in a comparison differences and common traits can be included. The ludic capacity implies a double view of reality, it combines perspectives. One application of the ludic capacity is therefore the art of handling contradictions, dichotomies and paradoxes. In scientific methodological terms the ludic represents an eclectic, poly-paradigmatic way of looking at reality. But examples also abound in daily life. It is possible to enjoy a movie and at the same time be conscious of how actors and director have done their job. On the one hand, participation and identification occur, on the other hand, one is constantly observing and reviewing what happens.

Even though participant observation is a *contradictio in terminis*, anthropologists make of simultaneity their trade mark. The participant observer's position represents continuity as well as rupture, identification as well as distance, both simultaneity and simulation. A seemingly contradictory procedure has proven to be a productive method. Perhaps one should not be too afraid of making a virtue of necessity. When discussing methodological theism, atheism and agnosticism, I referred to the distinction between scholars' positions in their practice of studying religion, and when speaking as private persons. This seeming contradiction may be positively valued as a symptom of the ludic capacity.

In the remainder of this chapter I will argue that the ludic, as a human capacity, can and should manifest itself in the scholarly study of religion, and moreover that it is fundamental to religion itself. I will also suggest that the 'double awareness' can be put to use to find a way beyond religionism and reductionism. This allows for a combination of two diverging positions, and adds the possibility of a meta-position.

INTERDISCIPLINARY VIEWS

Simultaneity and subjunctivity have been discussed in various, relatively diverging disciplines and schools of thought. In a playful manner, not hindered by seeming contradictions or monoparadigmatic and disciplinary scruples, I will now call my witnesses from these disciplines and schools to the box. The summary I give here reflects my rather haphazard and sometimes intuitive reading experience. I was amazed by the surprising similarity between seemingly divergent arguments. Despite their variety, all references reinforce the plea for the application of the ludic capacity, both in religion and in the study of religion. The perspective the Wagenia first showed to me, and that the Brazilian spiritists confirmed in their own way, can be pursued in the scholars' tribe.

My first witness is Maurice Bloch. He has recently (1991) drawn anthropologists' attention to connectionism – also called parallel distributed processing, PDP (D'Andrade 1992: 29; 1995: 138–49) – as a fundamental hypothesis about human thought. Whereas it has long been assumed that people think as they speak, i.e. in sentences, recent research suggests that people are able to appeal to different 'non-linguistic chunked mental models' (Bloch 1991: 194) at the same time, making up their minds within seconds, 'making it possible to carry out thousands of tiny computations simultaneously' (D'Andrade 1992: 29). Images are used as stores of information. Connectionists suggest that knowledge is made accessible 'through a number of processing units which work in parallel and feed in information simultaneously . . . the information received from these multiple parallel processors is analysed simultaneously through already existing networks connecting the processors' (Bloch 1991: 191). The simultaneity also means that dichotomies can be overcome. Once a conclusion has to be explained, sentential logic and dichotomous thinking take over again. Though they are much more visible and seemingly dominant, they do not represent the normal way of thinking.

Quinn and Holland (1987) have developed similar ideas. They coined the term 'cultural model' as a narrative, prototypical, schematic and simplified form of social knowledge that is available to interpret events. Quinn and Holland stress the simultaneity of a variety of cultural models used to perform tasks, both interpretative and goal-embodying, verbal and non-verbal, thinking and doing (ibid.: 6–8). Following Lakoff and Johnson, the authors distinguish between proposition-schemas and image-schemas (ibid.: 24, cf.

Quinn 1991: 58). The first type is based on what Bloch has called sentential logic, while the second illustrates the connectionist-PDP view of the way knowledge is organized. A key image, a root metaphor, often physical and bodily, can summarize knowledge in a way that is much more rapid than its explanation in propositions would be. This has methodological consequences, as Csordas (1993) has pointed out, suggesting 'somatic modes of attention' as an important instrument in research. The holistic perspective of the key image is complemented by the verbalization of propositional logic. One might perhaps add: the religious experience of inspiring images is complemented by the verbalizations of narrative in myth and of reason in theological – as well as atheist – discourse.

Translated in structuralist terms this can also be called the paradigmatic comparison of syntagmatic chains. Connectionist and image thought is paradigmatic, whereas sententional and propositional logic is syntagmatic in nature. The process of 'bricolage' combines the two types of view and makes them more dynamic. It is like hearing melody (contiguity) and harmony (analogy) at the same time, and improvising with them.

From cognitive anthropology we move on to psycho-analysis. An interesting way to illuminate the fundamental characteristics of simultaneity and subjunctivity in the ludic can be found in Winnicott (1971). Though psychoanalytic in origin, his interpretation of play is not as strictly Freudian as, for example, that given by Alexander (1958), who links play with libido. Winnicott takes his starting-point in the infant's discovery of the difference between 'me' and 'not-me', between subject and object (1971: 6). He suggests that between the two there is an intermediate area to which inner reality and external life contribute. The individual, also when adult, is 'engaged in the perpetual human task of keeping inner and outer reality separate yet interrelated' (ibid.: 2). Winnicott locates play in the intermediate area. 'Transitional objects', such as the modern infant's teddy bear, represent a bridge between inner experience and outer reality.

In Winnicott's view, illusions are also characteristic of the intermediate area, since the transitional object seems to be part of both inner reality and external life. Interestingly, 'illusion' is etymologically related to 'ludic', as Huizinga has observed (1952: 12). Winnicott considers the illusions to be non-pathological (1971: 15), even though the child gradually meets with disillusionment, weaning being the clearest example. Adults maintain their illusions, as in art and religion (Winnicott 1971: 3). Winnicott suggests a link between the infant's experience and collective culture. Transitional objects are instrumental in constructing this link.

Transitional objects provide the first experience of symbolism. The softness of the teddy bear represents the mother's breast, experienced by the infant as part of the body. Transitional objects also offer the first experience of power: 'The mother's adaptation to the infant's needs, when good enough, gives the infant the illusion that there is an external reality that corresponds to the infant's own capacity to create' (ibid.: 6). It gives the infant the confidence that there is 'a neutral area of experience which will not be challenged' (ibid.: 12). To adults, religion and art belong to this unchallenged intermediate area. They offer relief from the strain of relating inner and outer reality (ibid.: 13). 'The thing about playing is always the precariousness of the interplay of personal psychic reality and the experience of control of actual objects. This is the precariousness of magic itself' (ibid.: 47).

Winnicott's approach to play can be confirmed by contributions from symbolic and psychological anthropology. Ewing (1990) speaks of the 'illusion of wholeness'. She suggests that a person will always maintain this illusion, despite the presence of 'multiple inconsistent self-representations that are context-dependent and may shift rapidly' (ibid.: 251). People develop ways of managing inconsistencies (ibid.: 253). They are 'adept at using multiple rhetorical strategies, relying on ambiguity and tropes to establish a position' (ibid.: 262). As a consequence, cultures are not the coherent systems they have been assumed to be (ibid.: 257). This can also be put in connectionist terms: the chunked models of the self-representations can be simultaneously active, despite inconsistencies. Quinn and Holland put it this way:

> That there is no coherent cultural system of knowledge, only an array of different culturally shared schematizations formulated for the performance of particular cognitive tasks, accounts for the co-existence of the conflicting cultural models encountered in many domains of existence.
>
> (Quinn and Holland 1987: 10)

In my terms it is the human ludic capacity that allows for a satisfying management of inconsistencies, of the fundamental tension between consenting and diverging. Scientific thinking does not escape the co-existence of conflicting cultural models, but especially in eclectic approaches the multiplicity of views is recognized and becomes part of the method.

The analysis made by Winnicott and Ewing finds a parallel in the work of the Dutch anthropologist of religion Jan van Baal. Comparing play, art and religion, Van Baal (1972) points to a common source of these three sectors of culture. Human beings feel both part of the world and yet at a distance. Symbols cause that distance, because to the human subject, defined as *homo exprimens*, they refer to objects, even when these are not present. The capacity for reflection is paid for with distance, absence and loneliness.

In Van Baal's opinion, play, art and religion, each in its own way, offer a solution to the fundamental tension of being at the same time part of reality and at a distance from it (Van Baal 1972: 118). In *play* the participants create a separate world which they know to be fictitious. This world has its own rules, but despite these rules the uncertainty of chance is just as present. In *art* the world addresses the human being as essentially beautiful, as an invitation to enjoy reality. Thus it gives him or her a sense of belonging, of being part, even though the aesthetic experience may be momentary. *Religion* offers a solution to this fundamental problem by offering a possibility of communication, primarily with supernatural powers, but also with fellow human beings and with nature. The difference between the world evoked in play and that evoked in religion is that only in the latter do matters of life and death predominate. Whereas in the reality of play uncertainty is exciting, in that of religion uncertainty nourishes fear. Of the three categories discussed here, play offers the greatest awareness that one is dealing with an imaginary world, with an illusion that helps one to understand the incomprehensible mystery (ibid.: 125).

Victor Turner, who contributed to various sub-disciplines of anthropology, developed a special approach to the study of the ludic, particularly in his later publications. Yet, early in his career, when coining the concept of social drama, play was already central to his observations. This led him on to the study of ritual and theatre (Turner 1982). The liminary phase in the ritual process (Turner 1974) has many ludic characteristics, even though the initial list of typical liminary elements did not include play (1974: 93). In a later work Turner calls play the essence of liminality, and speaks of 'the ludic capacity, to catch symbols in their movement, so to speak, and to play with their possibilities of form and meaning' (1982: 23). Liminality combines work and play. In the modern 'liminoid' setting, play is exiled to the sphere of leisure, with the exception of some professionals, like academics and actors, who make their play a commercial activity (1982: 33, 55).

Turner's work is very tentative and conjectural; it is most stimulating for the study of play. In his view, play bridges the contrast between the two hemispheres of the human brain, the two being characterized by different tasks. Following Barbara Lex, Turner (1988: 163) describes as tasks of the left hemisphere: speech, linear analytic thought, assessment of time, sequentially organized information. The right hemisphere is characterized by: limited linguistic capability, holistic synthetic thought, perception of space, information organized in patterns. From D'Aquili, Laughlin and McManus (1979: 174), Turner takes the idea of a 'rapid functional alternation of each hemisphere' (quoted in Turner 1988: 164). The left half is dominant and activating, the right half has a stabilizing effect. One is of course reminded of Bloch's distinction between sentential logic and parallel distributed processing. The connectionist 'processing units' might be located in the right hemisphere, whereas verbalization can be said to take place in the left half. The structuralist distinction between paradigmatic comparisons and syntagmatic chains, or, in the musical metaphor, between harmony and melody, can also be included in this schema of the brain hemispheres.

Turner understands ritual as based on a combination of the two hemispheres' characteristics, producing a feeling of well-being. Ecstasy, mysticism, and enlightenment are terms for this state, in which paradoxes are considered acceptable or even welcome (1988: 166). Adding italics, Turner again quotes D'Aquili, Laughlin and McManus (1979: 177) who suggest that 'during certain ritual and meditation states, logical paradoxes or the awareness of polar opposites as presented in myth appear simultaneously, *both* as antinomies and as unified wholes'. In a later publication the same authors (Laughlin, McManus and D'Aquili 1990: 180) refer to play as 'at the very evolutionary foundations of both science and mysticism'. Turner affirms that play is difficult to localize in the brains. It has an inter-face function (Turner 1988: 167), 'betwixt and between', 'as if' rather than 'as is' (ibid.: 169).

Many of the insights that have been presented so far point to a link between the ludic and a fundamental human predicament: that of having to deal simultaneously with various forms of reality that make themselves felt all at the same time. This point has been pursued in symbolic anthropology. An interesting human instrument in dealing with this predicament is the trope, especially the tropes of metaphor and metonym. Tropes contain ludic aspects. They are used to get a grip on reality, to maintain the sensation of a unified, unfragmented reality. Fernandez speaks of the play of and between the tropes (1986, 1991: 6, 7); Friedrich introduces the term 'polytropy' (Friedrich 1991: 17–55).

Metaphors pertain to two domains (Quinn and Holland 1987: 30). They are images taken from a familiar domain and applied to another, inchoate (Fernandez 1986, *passim*) and unfamiliar domain, with the purpose of clarifying this latter domain and making it more familiar. Scholars also use metaphors, as when society is compared to an organism or a mechanism. Especially in religion, metaphors return the subject to the whole, precisely by establishing a relationship between two domains, all the more so because hitherto these seemed unconnected (Fernandez 1986: 118–213). There is a double perspective in metaphors: society may be an organism, but even to functionalists it was clear that, literally speaking, it is not so. As McFague (1983: 13) has observed, metaphors 'always contain the whisper, "it is *and it is not*" '. Bateson (1973: 158), when speaking of play, distinguishes between primary and secondary process thinking: primary in the sense that map and territory are equated, secondary when they are distinguished. Play in his view combines the two types of process thinking. In view of these observations, one might conclude that metaphors create illusions, but that these are useful illusions that are widely held and applied, also in science: 'scientific models can be construed as extended metaphors' (Edwards 1994: 180).

Of course, metaphors are not reinvented every time they are used. A speaker, using a metaphor, expects the audience to recognize the movement from two separate domains to two related domains or even one integrated domain (Fernandez 1986: 45). The ludic, as the capacity to deal simultaneously and subjunctively with two ways of classifying reality, finds in metaphors an important instrument for the routine connecting of these two orders.

Metonyms pertain to one domain instead of two, but lead to the same result. A particular experience or phenomenon within that domain is generalized for the whole of it. An example from religion is the Christian expression that 'the cross saves from sin', in which 'the cross' represents Jesus' death as well as a whole theological reasoning about his death. In the case of metonym, two levels of order, one partial and the other referring to a whole, are connected. This again illustrates the simultaneous double perspective of the ludic. So in both metaphor and metonym people play with domains and levels of order. They are engaged in 'the play of tropes in culture' (Fernandez 1986).

Metaphors and metonyms can be distinguished but occur together. If metaphors entail the suggestion of a unity, of one domain, despite linking two domains, they are closer to metonyms than the distinction at first seems to suggest. One should therefore not limit oneself to the study of metaphor, but look 'Beyond Metaphor' (Fernandez 1991). Again distance and contiguity are looked at simultaneously, within the context of culture. Fernandez (ibid.: 13), referring explicitly to reductionism, makes a plea for the combination of two approaches, one reductionist and distant, the other more poetic and participatory:

> . . . on the one hand, anthropological poetics challenges the dehumanization that lies in the reductionist tendencies of scientific formalization, while, on the other hand, scientific formalization forestalls the excessively extravagant and freewheeling intuitive interpretations that are a tendency in poetic approaches.

Poewe (1989: 375) has observed that 'While academia seems preoccupied with text and genre, and the rarefied world of metaphor, many at the grass roots level have returned to experience, "life", and a language empowered by metonyms.' Scholars will more readily use metaphors because their supposed scientific objectivity keeps them at a distance from what they study. In daily life and in religion, reality is experienced as one domain, and consequently metonyms are more fitting. In Van Baal's terms religion is a way of restoring unity and wholeness. From within religious experience, then, metonym seems a better instrument than metaphor, even though metaphors keep being used.

Yet, scholars cannot do without metonyms. Especially anthropologists need them, because the distinction between metaphor and metonym is paralleled by that between observation (suggesting distance) and participation (suggesting one reality), participant observation being, as we saw, the twin method characteristic of anthropology. Here too, the ludic is present, since fieldworkers have to manage two perspectives at the same time. They need to find an equilibrium between distant observation and intimate participation. While observing, they belong to two domains; while participating, they belong to one only. When only observing they cannot participate, and *vice versa*. Fieldworkers often report on the play-acting needed in such situations. They too experience Ewing's tension between multiple selves and the illusion of wholeness, and find a way to manage these contradictions.

Finally, another school of thought that is relevant to our theme must be called to witness. Postmodernism, whatever its value in retrospect may be, has made two contributions to a growing awareness of the ludic in academic work. First, playfulness has been mentioned as typical of postmodernists (Rosenau 1992: 117, 135; B. S. Turner 1990: 4, 5; 1991: xxi). Postmodernists have a special interest in language games and experiment with style and narrative knowledge (Sarup 1988: 120). As in the ludic subjunctive dealing with two different orders, postmodernists cherish contradictions, indeterminacy, paradoxes and inconsistencies. Criticism of the one meta-narrative leads to experiment and openness, with carnival as a leading metaphor (Rosenau 1992: 141). Yet, unity and wholeness have become suspect, and in that sense postmodernism is blind to the fundamental tension between distance and participation, plurality and unity. To me, the simultaneity in the ludic seems to be more interesting than the – in the end often rather cynical – preference for fragmentation.

A second contribution of postmodernism has perhaps been less purposeful and more ambiguous. It does not relate to the ludic, but primarily to religion and science. I am referring to the idea that the postmodern deconstruction of traditional scientific models has eroded the contrast between science and religion as forms of knowledge (Berry and Wernick 1992). When 'presence' is no longer a core concept and 'darker, more obscure ways of seeing and thinking' (Berry 1992: 2) become acceptable, that contrast loses much of its point. As Milbank puts it (1992: 31): 'one can no longer will the *end* of religion.'

Rorty, often mentioned in connection with postmodernism, introduces a term that comes close to the ludic. He speaks of the 'ironist' (1989: xv) as:

> . . . the sort of person who faces up to the contingency of his or her most central beliefs and desires – someone sufficiently historicist and nominalist to have abandoned the idea that those central beliefs and desires refer back to something beyond the reach of time and chance.

The ironist is opposed by Rorty to the theologian and the metaphysician. Since this ironism is linked to liberalism, the liberal being depicted as a person who thinks 'that cruelty is the worst thing we do' (Sklar quoted by Rorty 1989: xv), this posture is certainly not cynical. Compared to the ludic as defined above, it contains a certain degree of subjunctivity, but lacks the simultaneity of combining, for example, ironist and metaphysical points of view. Whereas Rorty's ironist is ironical about a foundation beyond time and chance, someone who is ironic in the ludic way will underline a double understanding, of both the 'either' and the 'or'.

Our witnesses, though drawn from such diverse approaches and disciplines as cognitive studies, psycho-analysis, symbolic anthropology, anthropology of religion, neurobiology and postmodernism, all point to the possibility of a subjunctivity and simultaneity in points of view.

THE LUDIC, RELIGION, AND THE EXPLANATION OF RELIGION

As we have seen above, the debate on reductionism and religionism suggests the need of a choice between different ways of classifying reality. The questions formulated in that section point to a series of tenacious contrasts, such as between rational and irrational orders, the religious and the scientific way of classifying, the believers' and the scholars' classifications, Western and non-Western views. They also refer to differing concepts of science.

It has already been observed that the sharpness of these contrasts has been somewhat eroded in the last decades. In the light of the preceding section, it seems to me that awareness of the ludic human potential reinforces this tendency and gives it a new basis, since it points to the art of simultaneously and subjunctively dealing with contrasting classifications. The various types of explanation of religion, even though contrasting and exclusive among themselves, can be valued in a ludic approach. Thus it will be possible to go beyond the familiar dichotomies, not necessarily by producing a synthesis or some form of dialectics, but by the simultaneous adoption of two or more perspectives. To their own disadvantage, scholars have left an essential part of the human potential unused. Academics may reflect the modernity of the time they live in, but they also suffer from the consequences of the modern exile of the ludic, domesticated in its own harmless sphere. They have to learn anew how to use both hemispheres of their brain at the same time, and thus to handle dichotomies.

If the ludic simultaneity has recently been recovered and rediscovered, this human talent should not be buried, but put to use. More than anywhere else, the study of religion is an area where it can be applied, not only because of its relevance for methodology, but also because religion is one of the areas where the ludic is at work. I suggest that methodological ludism is necessary to study the ludic capacity of religious people. Object and method happen to be based on the same foundation, and this is more than a mere coincidence. This similarity between the simultaneity of views in religion and in the study of religion presents itself for the simple reason that the ludic capacity can be applied to more than one field of human activity. The implementation of ludism as a meta-position in scholarly work opens the scholar's eyes to the believer's 'constellation' view.

This posture takes us beyond the choice between methodological atheism, agnosticism, or theism. In appealing to a perspective of simultaneity, the ludic invites one to take a triple view, at the same time theist, atheist and agnosticist. In this way methodological theism, so far neglected in the debate, can be given a place. Van Baal's legacy, expressed in his last publication (1990: 20, 55), urging us to consider the believer as normal and not as deviant, can then be elaborated. The anthropologist's method of participant observation offers a good starting-point if interpreted as a ludic activity in the sense I have given to the word (cf. ibid.: 55). If only as a hypothesis, scholars should invert the current perspective and start at the believer's end, taking the Mystery not as an option but as an obliging necessity (ibid.: 67). In this light, the idea of a 'useful illusion' is no longer a contradiction, but acceptable within the simultaneity of the ludic perspective (cf. Kliever 1981; Nijssen 1991; Vaihinger 1922).

As a method, the application of the ludic capacity to the study of religion is more than a juxtaposition of opposing approaches like those mentioned in the first paragraph of this section. It allows for a new way of looking at religion. The methodological ludism advocated here offers the extra of a simultaneous view. This is not necessarily a synthesis, but much more an overview of the total constellation of possibilities. It is also more than empathy, since the subjunctive 'make-believe' guarantees a serious sympathy that is honest and absolute as long as it lasts. In that sense ludism goes beyond the religionist and reductionist positions.

The use of the ludic capacity, which is recommended for the study and explanation of religion, can also be encountered in religion itself. If indeed it is a universal human capacity, it must necessarily be present in the religious field as well. Van Baal's remarks on the closeness between religion and play point in this direction, as does Fernandez's emphasis on the play of tropes and the quest for wholeness in religions (Fernandez 1986: 188–213). The human and the superhuman, nature and the supernatural, the part and the whole, as different orders, are simultaneously and subjunctively present in the ludic capacity as it is at work in religion.

There are several other indications that the ludic and the religious are related, as in ritual, especially through the use of masks, but also in myth, as in the trickster figure. Huizinga has already drawn attention to this (1952: *passim*). Syncretism can be defined as a ludic way of dealing with religious classifications of a different order. The same can be said of popular religion – often syncretistic – as an alternative to official religion. Magic represents an alternative, illegitimate production of religion (Bourdieu 1971). It can be understood within the ludic perspective, as was affirmed by Winnicott's phrase quoted above about the ambiguity between 'personal psychic reality and the experience of control of actual objects' and its link with the precariousness of magic. As Luhrmann (1989: 332–3) puts it, following Winnicott:

> The crucial part of magical practice is that the play-claim of being a powerful, efficacious magician is also a reality-claim, a science-like assertion about the objective instrumental efficacy of magic within the physical world.

This allows magicians 'to waver between the literal and the metaphorical when casting a spell' (Luhrmann 1989: 333). Perhaps students of religion should put a bit more of this magic into their study of religion!

It must be added that, as has occurred in the academic world, religions have often abolished the ludic dimension as disturbing. The subjunctive 'as if' is experienced as threatening. Simultaneity may be promising, but it is a menace to vested interests and to the sentential logical order of authorities. Therefore syncretism, magic, and popular religion are condemned by erudite religion as heresies. In this context it should be noted that doubt and scepsis are rarely part of the official version of a religion, even though they are typical of much religious experience, representing the ludic's double awareness. As Pruyser (1976: 190) affirms:

> Though the focal feelings may convince the participant that he is in the presence of the Holy, there may be a dim but persistent feeling in the background of his consciousness that he is involved in an act of "make-believe" and that it is perfectly within his powers to step out of it.

The Wagenia initiation is, as we saw, a perfect example of this 'make-believe'. In a similar manner the Brazilian spiritists created their own healing method.

Without idealizing the individual consciousness, it must be observed that in religion, as in science, institutionalization may generate power mechanisms. Whereas in science a process of monoparadigmatic school formation is the consequence, in religion fundamentalism and orthodoxy come to the fore. The connectionist mechanisms in religious thought are totally overlooked, and as a consequence one is blind to the ludic perspective. Metaphors are reified and taken literally. In Bateson's terms: map and territory are equated. What remains is the exclusively serious, verbalized and dichotomized sentential logic of orthodoxy, made for eternity, but in fact nothing more than a petrified monument of the past.

As far as science is concerned, the ludic posture demands what many would consider a literal *salto mortale*, the death of scientific explanation and debate. Yet, the special attractiveness of the ludic is the possibility to look at things from another angle, without abandoning a prior way of classifying that is considered preferable and even exclusive. The seriousness that is part of the ludic allows for both exclusiveness and inclusiveness. It is a way of playing with alternatives in which one can become captivated by each of these alternatives. It is the seduction of the metaphor that whispers 'it is *and it is not*' (McFague 1983: 13). It is a way of transforming the vice of contradiction into a methodological principle. The multiple selves of the researcher are complemented by the illusion of wholeness.

In terms of explanatory paradigms, a plea for the ludic therefore implies some form of eclecticism. The advantage of such an approach is that the space for creativity and experiment is enlarged, and in that sense the scientific enterprise need not succumb to the *salto mortale*, but appears rejuvenated. The ludic posture may, for example, put an end to a sterile exchange of arguments about the rationality of religion or of non-Western cultures. The self-sufficiency and inner logic of each way of classifying reality can be recognized without leading to a sterile relativism. It is the condition of simultaneity, instead of co-existence, that prevents relativism. In that manner the ludic also points to a way beyond a choice between objectivity and subjectivity. Secularization can be reconsidered in the light of the ludic perspective, interestingly not only from a scholarly point of view, but even in a personal way (Kliever 1981).

To elaborate on the methodological consequences would require another chapter. A new methodology must be developed, and this will certainly not be easy. The ludic capacity has some trickiness, is a trickster itself, as V. Turner (1988: 167–70) put it. Therefore its extra dimension escapes categories and makes for surprises. Yet, in scholarly work, something like Winnicott's intermediate area would be most helpful. It demands another way of looking and understanding, different from what scholars have been trained to do. The ludic offers a most promising perspective. Ludicity, though inevitably ludicrous to some, may lead to lucidity for others. One condition is that one forgets the over-serious 'official' view of religion that is often typical of Western culture and academic discourse, and also that one avoids the homogeneous univocal discourse on other cultures of the type 'The Bongo-Bongo are of the opinion that . . . '. Non-Western cultures and religions abound with examples of the ludic, as the Wagenia and their presumed secrets showed me when I started doing anthropological fieldwork. If the field of study is replete with examples, and if the double perspective required of the fieldworker is paralleled by that of religion, it should not be too difficult to adopt a corresponding methodology. It may mean that research reports have to avoid an excessively strict sentential logic. Since the publication of 'Writing Culture' (Clifford and Marcus 1986), anthropologists have more than ever been made aware of the 'poetics and politics of ethnography', in the words of the sub-title of that collection of articles. Awareness of styles will help to translate the ludic capacity into fieldwork methodology. With regard to politics, Wagenia novices and Brazilian spiritists have shown me the localized and political nature of my discourse. They called my attention to the ludic that had been exiled from my own discipline and that as a consequence I had been conditioned not to observe.

If ludism proves to be a viable alternative, the polemics between religionists and reductionists can gradually be brought to a conclusion. The interdisciplinary study of religion will be relieved of a cumbersome burden and can be immensely stimulated.

CONCLUSION

If students of religion integrate the human ludic capacity into their method, and discover its marks in the religions they study, the interdisciplinary study of religion will make a leap forward. The perspective of methodological ludism and of the simultaneity of classifications will make it possible to maintain personal convictions and at the same time accept those of others. In such a way one can be a believer and a student of other people's beliefs. It will be possible to use preferred methods without abandoning other methodologies. One can be a methodological theist, atheist and agnosticist at the same time and even add to these positions. An eclectical use of paradigms will no longer be something to be ashamed of. Interdisciplinary contact will be greatly facilitated. As proponents of the method of participant observation, anthropologists are in an excellent position to play a leading role in developing this liminary – or even preliminary – approach.

ACKNOWLEDGEMENTS

I want to thank Lourens Minnema for important reading suggestions; Anton van Harskamp, Bert Musschenga and the other members of the Relativism group of the Bezinningscentrum of the Vrije Universiteit, Amsterdam for their comments; Rein Fernhout, Sander Griffioen, Hans Tennekes, Henk Versnel and an anonymous reviewer for observations on earlier drafts; the members of the 'Specialisatieoverleg Religieuze en Symbolische Antropologie' and the 'Post-doc leesgroep' for their interest in my efforts to understand religion in a playful manner. I am grateful to the Research Centre for Religion and Society of the University of Amsterdam, especially Peter van Rooden, for a stimulating discussion. Special thanks to my Ph.D. students. As long as I have been reflecting on the ludic, João Guilherme Biehl has stimulated me immensely in continuing the quest for play.

REFERENCES

Alexander, F. (1958) 'A contribution to the theory of play', *Psychoanalytic Quarterly* 27; 175–93.

Bateson, G. (1973) 'A theory of play and fantasy', in G. Bateson, *Steps to an Ecology of Mind, Collected Essays in Anthropology, Psychiatry, Evolution and Epistemology*, St. Albans: Paladin, 150–66.

Berry, P. (1992) 'Introduction', in P. Berry and A. Wernick (eds), *Shadow of Spirit, Postmodernism and Religion*, London: Routledge, 1–8.

Berry, P. and A. Wernick (eds) (1992) *Shadow of Spirit, Postmodernism and Religion*, London: Routledge.

Bloch, M. (1991) 'Language, anthropology and cognitive science', *Man* 26: 183–98.

Bourdieu, P. (1971) 'Genèse et structure du champ religieux', *Revue Française de Sociologie* 12: 295–334.

Clarke, P. and P. Byrne (1993) *Religion Defined and Explained*, London: Macmillan.

Clifford, J. and G. E. Marcus (eds) (1986) *Writing Culture, The Poetics and Politics of Ethnography*, Berkeley: University of California Press.

Csordas, T. J. (1993) 'Somatic modes of attention', *Cultural Anthropology*, 8(2): 135–56.

D'Andrade, Roy G. (1992) 'Schemas and Motivation', in R. D'Andrade and C. Strauss (eds) *Human Motives and Cultural Models*, Cambridge: Cambridge University Press, 23–44.

—— (1995) *The Development of Cognitive Anthropology*, Cambridge: Cambridge University Press.

D'Aquili, E., C. D. Laughlin, and J. McManus (eds) (1979) *The Spectrum of Ritual*, New York: Columbia University Press.

Droogers, A. (1980) *The Dangerous Journey: Symbolic Aspects of Boys' Initiation among the Wagenia of Kisangai, Zaire*, Hague: Mouton.

—— (1991) 'Brazil as a Patient: Political Healing and "New Age" in a Spiritist Group', in André Droogers, Gerrit Huizer and Hans Siebers (eds), *Popular Power in Latin American Religions*, Saarbrücken and Fort Lauderdale: Breitenbach, 237–59.

Edwards, T. (1994) 'Religion, Explanation, and the Askesis of Inquiry', in T. A. Idinopulos and E. A. Yonan (eds), *Religion and Reductionism, Essays on Eliade, Segal, and the Challenge of the Social Sciences for the Study of Religion*, Leiden: Brill, 162–82.

Ehrmann, J. (1968) 'Homo Ludens Revisited', *Yale French Studies* 41: 31–57.

Ewing, K. P. (1990) 'The illusion of wholeness: culture, self, and the experience of inconsistency' *Ethos* 18(3): 251–78.

Fernandez, J. W. (1986) *Persuasions and Performances, The Play of Tropes in Culture*, Bloomington: Indiana University Press.

—— (ed.) (1991) *Beyond Metaphor, The Theory of Tropes in Anthropology*, Stanford CA: Stanford University Press.

Friedrich, P. (1991) 'Polytropy', in J.W. Fernandez (ed.), *Beyond Metaphor, The Theory of Tropes in Anthropology*, Stanford CA: Stanford University Press, 17–55.

Guthrie, S. E. (1993) *Faces in the Clouds, A New Theory of Religion*, New York, Oxford: Oxford University Press.

Huizinga, J. (1952) *Homo ludens, Proeve eener bepaling van het spel-element der cultuur*, Haarlem: Tjeenk Willink.

Idinopulos, T. A. and E. A. Yonan (eds) (1994) *Religion and Reductionism, Essays on Eliade, Segal, and the Challenge of the Social Sciences for the Study of Religion*, Leiden: Brill.

Kliever, L. D. (1981) 'Fictive religion: rhetoric and play', *The Journal of the American Academy of Religion* 49: 657–69.

Lacerda de Azevedo, José (1988) *Espírito/Matéria: Novos horizontes para a medicina*, Porto Alegre: Pallotti.

Laughlin, C. D., J. McManus, and E. D. D'Aquili (1990) *Brain, Symbol & Experience, Toward a Neurophenomenology of Human Consciousness*, Boston and Shaftesbury: New Science Library, Shambala.

Luhrmann, T. M. (1989) *Persuasions of the Witch's Craft: Ritual Magic and Witchcraft in Present-day England*, Oxford: Basil Blackwell.

McFague, S. (1983) *Metaphorical Theology*, London: SCM.

Milbank, J. (1992) 'Problematizing the secular: the post-postmodern agenda', in P. Berry and A. Wernick (eds), *Shadow of Spirit, Postmodernism and Religion*, London: Routledge, 30–44.

Nijssen, F. N. M. (1991) 'Onder goden en goochelaars' in *Trouw*, 15.2.91, p. 19.

Pannenberg, W. (1984) *Anthropologie in theologischer Perspektive*, Göttingen: Vandenhoeck & Ruprecht.

Poewe, K. (1989) 'On the metonymic structure of religious experiences: the example of charismatic Christianity', *Cultural Dynamics* 2 (4): 361–80.

Preus, J. S. (1987) *Explaining Religion, Criticism and Theory from Bodin to Freud*, New Haven and London: Yale University Press.

Pruyser, P. W. (1976) *A Dynamic Psychology of Religion*, New York: Harper & Row.

Quinn, N. (1991) 'The cultural basis of metaphor', in J.W. Fernandez (ed.), *Beyond Metaphor, The Theory of Tropes in Anthropology*, Stanford, California: Stanford University Press, 56–93.

Quinn, N. and D. Holland (eds) (1987) *Cultural Models in Language and Thought*, Cambridge: Cambridge University Press.

Rorty, R. (1989) *Contingency, Irony, and Solidarity*, Cambridge: Cambridge University Press.

Rosenau, P. M. (1992) *Post-Modernism and the Social Sciences: Insights, Inroads, and Intrusions*, Princeton, New Jersey: Princeton University Press.

Sarup, M. (1988) *An Introductory Guide to Post-structuralism and Postmodernism*, New York: Harvester Wheatsheaf.

Segal, R. A. (1989) *Religion and the Social Sciences: Essays on the Confrontation*, Atlanta GA: Scholars Press.

Sharpe, E. J. (1975) *Comparative Religion: A History*, London: Duckworth.

Thomas, L.-V., R. Luneau and J.-L. Doneux (1969) *Les religions d'Afrique Noire: Textes et traditions sacrés*, Paris: Fayard Denoël.

Turner, Bryan S. (ed.) (1990) *Theories of Modernity and Postmodernity*, London: Sage.

—— (1991) (ed.) *Religion and Social Theory*, London: Sage.

Turner, V. (1974) *The Ritual Process, Structure and Anti-structure*, Harmondsworth: Penguin.

—— (1982) *From Ritual to Theatre: The Human Seriousness of Play*, New York: PAJ Publications.

—— (1988) *The Anthropology of Performance*, New York: PAJ Publications.

Vaihinger, H. (1922) *Die Philosophie des Als ob, System der theoretischen, praktischen und religiösen Fiktionen der Menschheit auf Grund eines idealistischen Positivismus*, Leipzig: Felix Meiner.

Van Baal, J. (1972) *De boodschap der drie illusies, Overdenkingen over religie, kunst en spel*, Assen: Van Gorcum.

—— (1990) *Mysterie als openbaring*, Utrecht: ISOR.

Winnicott, D. W. (1971) *Playing and Reality*, London: Tavistock.

4

MULTIPLE IMAGES OF ETHNIC REALITY

Beyond Disagreement?

Peter Kloos

Edmundo Magaña's Ph.D. thesis, an ethnography of the Caribs in Surinam, entitled *Orión y la mujer Pléyades, Simbolismo astronómico de los indios kaliña de Surinam* was published in 1988. Although the book at first sight seems to deal with a subject of limited scope, namely Carib astronomy, it is much more than that. In it, names of stellar constellations are explained in terms of myth, and myth is in a variety of ways embedded in a social structure, based on the position of men and women vis-à-vis each other, and in a subsistence economy. A good deal of Magaña's account therefore deals with mundane facts of terrestrial life rather than with celestial phenomena. Ethnographically speaking the book is based on already published accounts of the Caribs and on Magaña's fieldwork in 1980 and 1985–6. Theoretically the thesis is to a large extent informed by Lévi-Straussian structuralism.

One of Magaña's published sources of ethnographic detail is my own Ph.D. thesis, *The Maroni River Caribs of Surinam*, published in 1971. This monograph deals with the evolution of Carib society, including the ways Carib village structure and its culture have become integrated in colonial, later post-colonial Surinam society. As an ethnography the book is almost entirely based on fieldwork in two Carib villages on the lower Maroni River in the period 1966–8. Theoretically it is informed by what Marvin Harris in 1968 had called cultural materialism (Harris 1968).

The remarkable thing is that for the naïve reader the two ethnographies seem to deal with different societies and cultures, not with the same twin-villages Christiaankondre and Langamankondre, together known as Galibi. The explanation of the difference is, of course, the difference in theoretical perspective. For Magaña, social life is an enactment of cosmological notions. For me, social structure is the outcome of specific features of technology and division of labour. This difference gives rise, understandably, to markedly different interpretations, even different 'facts'. For example, during the period of my stay among the Maroni River Caribs I counted eighteen shamans (*pïyei*) among the adult men, and I found that their distribution in settlements coincided with the various localized kinship groups, who in this way were medically/religiously self-sufficient (Kloos 1968; 1971: 209ff.). According to

Magaña, however, *all* Carib men are shamans: as hunters in their relation to the spirits of the forest (Magaña 1988: 193ff.).

Whose account is a reader going to believe? And for what reasons? What is the relationship between the two accounts of the same society and culture, or rather, what is the significance of having two different accounts? What is the meaning of 'truth' in this respect?

Until quite recently the issue of ethnographic discrepancies and of ethnographic truth was largely an academic one. Today, however, the representation of cultural reality has acquired a new, and rather volatile meaning. In a world that is slowly evolving towards a global economic, political and cultural world order, local cultural identities are surprisingly strongly emphasized – so much so that in many states, people regarding themselves as an ethnic entity are demanding more autonomy and sometimes even political independence. So-called 'ethnic civil war' is often the result of demands for more autonomy and the refusal of state governments to grant this (cf. Kloos 1993). 'Ethnic identity' is a strategic concept here, and anthropology has a lot to offer as far as ethnic identities are concerned. In such a context, however, ethnic identity is no longer a neutral fact, but a construct people are willing to fight for. Precisely because it is a construct, ethnic identity is highly problematic: ethnicities felt to be very old may in fact be historically very young. A motherland today felt as an ancient and inalienable right may have been absent a generation ago. In such a context the question of who is right and who is wrong acquires a sinister reality. For actors in these ethnic dramas, right and wrong are politically not scientifically defined. Antagonists are dealt with accordingly: they may even be killed (cf. Kloos 1995 on Sri Lanka). How do anthropologists deal with these differences in rendering of ethnic realities?

ETHNOGRAPHIES, ETHNOGRAPHERS AND ANTHROPOLOGISTS

An ethnography is a description of a particular society and its culture, or part of a society and its sub-culture. Ethnography predates anthropology as a recognized discipline. Many ethnographic accounts have been written by travellers, conquistadors, administrators, and missionaries. They were usually not trained in scientific research, and certainly not in anthropology. Their descriptions are often very unsystematic, or are characterized by a systematization of their own finding. In the *Encyclopaedie der Karaiben*, written by the Roman Catholic missionary W. Ahlbrinck, and one of the early descriptions of Carib society and culture in Surinam, for instance, ethnographic data are alphabetically ordered, with *Carib* vocabulary as point of departure (Ahlbrinck 1931).

However, since the time of Franz Boas and Bronislaw Malinowski, the founders of modern anthropology in the United States and in England respectively, *anthropological* ethnographic accounts are based on lengthy and intensive research by theoretically trained scholars, who to some extent participate in a society to observe what people are actually doing and thinking. In this way, the so-called fieldworkers are expected to present a factually accurate as well as a theoretically informed description of a specific way of life. Yet these descriptions of specific ways of life may disagree, as the example of the Caribs suggests, and this article is about these multiple and apparently conflicting images of the same society and culture – sometimes even the same village society and its culture, as is the case with Magaña's image of the Maroni River Caribs and my own account.

The first clear case of such a controversy to reach the anthropological media was probably that of the Zuñi, which pitched the well-known American anthropologist Ruth Benedict against a young Chinese scholar, Li An-Che. In 1934, Benedict published her *Patterns of Culture*. It is probably one of the most widely read anthropological studies. The main theme of her book is the ruling motivation of a culture. In this work, she contrasts the sober, highly disciplined Zuñi Indians with the exuberant Kwakiutl of the American northwest coast as well as with the Indians of the Plains. A few years later Li An-Che, a young Chinese scholar from Peking University, spent three months among the Zuñi. He saw many things of which Benedict apparently had not seen: emotionally charged prayers, marital trouble and conflict. Where Benedict had seen a highly integrated culture based on such values as equanimity, modesty and cooperation, Li An-Che saw tension, suspicion and ambition (Li An-Che 1937).

Because Benedict and Li An-Che had carried out their research in the same *pueblo* or village, cultural variation as an explanation of these differences can be ruled out. Because there were only a few years between the two periods of research, change as an explanation can in all likelihood also be ruled out. Was one of them simply wrong? It is not that simple. The discrepancy between these two representations of the Zuñi is not restricted to the work of Benedict and Li An-Che. Observers of Zuñi (and to some extent also of the closely related Hopi and other so-called Pueblo Indians) seem to stress *either* overt harmony *or* hidden tension. Apparently the discrepancies are related to some systematic perceptional difference between scholars.

RESTUDIES

Li An-Che's research would today be called a *restudy*. The first scholar to actually use the term 'restudy' was, as far as I know, Oscar Lewis when he called a book based on fieldwork in Mexico *Life in a Mexican Village: Tepoztlán Restudied* (1951). Tepoztlán is a village in the Mexican state of Morelos. An earlier scholar, Robert Redfield, had carried out research in Tepoztlán in 1926 and 1927. His book, *Tepoztlán. A Mexican Village* (1930), is one of the first studies of what later came to be known as peasant societies. Tepoztlán became famous only after Oscar Lewis's research there in 1943. A historian by training, Lewis turned to anthropology and went to Mexico to assist in programmes aimed at improving the quality of life in Mexican Indian communities. In this context he choose Tepoztlán because the earlier work by Redfield offered him a base line from which to measure and analyse change (Lewis 1951: xiii). Yet while working in Tepoztlán, Lewis became convinced that the picture which Redfield had painted was biased. Redfield had described a harmonious community of people who worked collectively rather than individually. Lewis stressed individuality and distrust in interpersonal relations as well as conflict.

An important difference between the Zuñi controversy and the Tepoztlán one is that Redfield and Lewis entered into a discussion about the background to the differences in their perceptions of reality. As far as I know, Benedict never commented in print on Li An-Che's findings. The latter returned to China in 1936 (even before the publication of his article). He never resumed his American studies, turning to Tibetan society and culture instead.

The latest major discrepancy regards William Foot Whyte's famous study *Street Corner Society* (1943), a study of an Italian slum in an American city (Boston). *Street Corner Society* has had a tremendous impact on sociology and social psychology, but in a lengthy article published in 1992, Marianne Boelen argues that Whyte, due to his ignorance of Italian culture, misrepresented what he saw among the migrants, that he was preoccupied with negative aspects of *Street Corner Society*, and that he even had distorted basic facts (Boelen 1992: 11–51). This was a serious accusation, concerning an almost sacrosanct book. The *Journal of Contemporary Ethnography* devoted a whole issue (21(1) 1992) to this controversy, in which Whyte defended himself, and others defended Whyte (see also Bovenkerk 1992).

In anthropology, the latest major controversy regards Samoa. Here Margaret Mead carried out her highly influential work on adolescence, published in *Coming of Age in Samoa* (1928). In 1983 Freeman published his *Margaret Mead and Samoa. The Making and Unmaking of an Anthropological Myth*, in which he argued that virtually all statements Mead ever made regarding Samoa were wrong! His book led to prolonged and heated discussions. The Samoa controversy is intriguing because as early as 1954 the American anthropologist Holmes went to Samoa and to the village in which Mead had carried out her fieldwork. He worked with those of her informants who were still alive and 'systematically investigated and evaluated every word that Mead wrote in *Coming of Age in Samoa* (1928), *Social Organization of Manu'a* (1930) and several articles' (Holmes 1983: 929). Contrary to Freeman, Holmes found Mead to be largely correct (Holmes 1957; 1987).

Freeman relates in his book that he had handed over the manuscript to Mead and corresponded about it, but Mead died before it was published and unless Freeman decides to make available the letters they exchanged we will never know her point of view (cf. Bateson 1984). The Mead–Freeman controversy reached major newspapers in the United States and also in Europe, probably because it threw doubt upon the scientific work of such an eminent scholar as Margaret Mead.

Although every fieldworker comments on the reliability of available data, Holmes seems to be the first researcher (and to my knowledge the only one) to make the attempt systematically to verify an earlier study in anthropology. It therefore comes close to what is technically called *replication*.

Between the 1937 article by Li An-Che, and Freeman's violent attack on Mead in 1983 there are many more cases of discrepancies similar to Zuñi, Tepoztlán, and Samoa. Still, given the high number of ethnographic accounts that have been published in recent years the number of serious discrepancies is not very high. In an earlier publication on restudies I listed nineteen examples (Kloos 1988a: 131). My present list covers a total number of more than thirty twin studies showing major discrepancies. (Of course, there are many more cases of minor disagreements between fieldworkers who worked in the same society and culture.) The explanation of this relatively low number seems to be that fieldworkers until recently generally avoided doing research where a colleague had already carried out fieldwork. Fieldworkers do not consciously seek conflict over their ethnographic accounts (for reasons see Kloos 1994).

WHAT ETHNOGRAPHY IS ABOUT

Handbooks on method in anthropology pay surprisingly little attention to ethnographic controversies, because these controversies may point out a basic unreliability in anthropological fieldwork. At stake, after all, is the relationship between reality and description – one of the major issues of scientific methodology. In a world in which scientific research has become such a dominant force this is a serious issue. The issue is more complicated today than some thirty years ago, when most anthropologists cherished rather naïve positivist ideas about the nature of ethnographic research.

What do fieldworkers do when they write ethnography? Do they pretend to represent reality? Or is their writing just one of a multitude of possible images of reality? *Has* it anything to do with reality? The discussion about the reliability and the validity of ethnographic facts is an old one. Before the rise of modern, fieldwork-based anthropology, the majority of anthropologists, whether professionals or laymen, were armchair scholars who developed their theories on the basis of ethnographic data collected and published by others. Early in the nineteenth century the low reliability of the data was already realized. The efforts of the early nineteenth-century anthropologists eventually resulted in the practice of fieldwork as we know it today (cf. Stocking 1983). The first generation of monographs, with their unprecedented wealth of detailed information, subdued at least for the time being uneasy feelings about the trustworthiness of the data.

The discussion of the reliability and validity of ethnography was resumed in the 1960s and gained momentum in the 1970s and 1980s, when postmodernism also acquired a foothold in anthropology. Recent history of anthropology saw changes in opinion even among staunch empiricists. The British anthropologist Edmund Leach, for instance, argued in 1984 that:

> . . . the data which derive from fieldwork are subjective not objective. I am saying that every anthropological observer . . . will see something that no other such observer can recognize, namely a kind of harmonious projection of the observer's own personality.
>
> (Leach 1984: 22)

Leach went on arguing that anthropological texts can be read in two different ways. They can be read as texts that are interesting in themselves, full of hidden meanings, but without assuming that 'what is discussed in the text corresponds to any kind of "reality" ' (1984: 22). Or they can be read 'with the set purpose of discovering projections of the author's personality, or of finding a record of how he or she reacted to what was going on' (Leach 1984: 22).

That this point of view was not a mere whim set on paper in a requested article for the *Annual Review of Anthropology* is demonstrated by Leach's review of Geertz's *Works and Lives: The Anthropologist as Author*. Leach concludes his review by saying that 'Ethnographers as authors are not primarily concerned with factual truth' (Leach 1989: 141).

Although the rather firmly entrenched positivist tradition in anthropology is nowadays challenged by a constructivist point of view (see Kloos 1988b), few anthropologists, I believe, would subscribe to such an extreme position as Leach's. The majority of fieldworkers are concerned with 'factual truth' of a kind. Although Leach is right in stressing that fieldworkers see things that no other observer will recognize, I would, contra Leach, equally stress that different observers often manage to see things the same way, and in any case are able to recognize each other's descriptions and make use of them. Although there are serious ethnographic discrepancies, there are also many cases, and certainly far more than thirty, of anthropological fieldworkers coming from widely different backgrounds who nonetheless arrive at descriptions that *do not* conflict. Such cases argue against extreme relativism, solipsism or postmodernism, or whatever designation one would like to use. The case of the Minankabau in Sumatra, Indonesia provides an excellent example. Fieldworkers from the Netherlands, England, Japan, Switzerland, the United States, as well as from Indonesia, have worked here – male and female. Although this would provide an ideal situation for multiple, widely divergent and even conflicting images of the 'same' reality, until now no serious discrepancies have surfaced. It would be worthwhile to find out why this is so.

So, the challenge – how to deal with differences between fieldworkers describing the same society and culture in conflicting terms – is there. It is a serious one; after all, the credibility of anthropology is at stake. In this article I will, first, classify the sources of ethnographic disagreement, and then, after having discarded the more spurious ones, concentrate on the most serious single source, namely contrasting theoretical orientations characterizing present-day anthropology.

WHY ETHNOGRAPHERS DISAGREE

By and large, there are four possible explanations why ethnographers disagree (see Heider 1988; Kloos 1988a). The disagreements may be due to:

1 cultural variation within one and the same society
2 sociocultural change
3 errors of observation and fraud
4 differences in research perspective.

A combination of these factors is, of course, possible. Let me illustrate these explanations by summarizing a few concrete cases.

CULTURAL VARIATION WITHIN ONE SOCIETY

One explanation of disagreement between two fieldworkers lies in intra-societal variation. Although the fieldworkers concerned appear to have carried out their researches in the 'same' society, what they describe are in fact different *versions* of the same society. However, a summary review of the cases makes immediately clear that this explanation can cover only a very small minority of the ethnographic controversies. In many cases of restudy, research is carried out in exactly the same community. (In Samoa, Holmes even used the same informants as Mead!) This choice is usually a deliberate one because the objective of the research is to study changes that have taken place since the first observations were made by fieldworkers. Still, there is sometimes room for doubt, even in the case of the Mead–Freeman controversy regarding Samoa. Mead carried out her research in one particular village in American Samoa; Freeman uses data coming from all islands of the Samoan archipelago and from all periods. There are good reasons to assume that Samoa was culturally not homogeneous (the Samoans of the small island where Mead carried out her fieldwork were known to be more conservative than those of the bigger islands).

In 1976, there was a debate concerning the degree of nomadism among the Brazilian Nambikwara, a society that had been studied by Lévi-Strauss in 1938, with far-reaching consequences for the theoretical points of view he was about to develop. Certain characteristics of their society and culture became key elements of his ideas regarding dualism and binary opposition – central issues of his version of structuralism (see Lévi-Strauss 1955, 1963). His portrayal of the Nambikwara was challenged by later fieldworkers, among them Aspelin, who argued that the Nambikwara were sedentary (Aspelin 1976, 1978, 1979). However, there is a real possibility that Lévi-Strauss worked with an atypical, marginal subgroup of Nambikwara who were truly nomadic (see Kloos 1988a: 73–82).

SOCIOCULTURAL CHANGE

Disagreement between fieldworkers can also be attributed to cyclical or structural change. For self-evident reasons, restudies take place at a later time than the original ones meaning that omnipresent processes of change may have substantially altered a society and its culture. The second fieldworker is usually quite aware of substantial change. Indeed, that is often what he or she is trying to study by restudying an already known community. Still, there is a strange twist here because the second fieldworker may become convinced that his or her colleague was wrong even with regard to the time the fieldwork was done. On the other hand, the second fieldworker may overlook the effects of changes noted. Discussing the discrepancies between Lewis's account of Tepoztlán and his own, Redfield stresses their complementarity. In contrasting accounts of a community he saw a means to better understanding and pleaded in favour of the deliberate construction of complementary descriptions (Redfield 1960: 132–3). He argued that the difference in the case of Tepoztlán was due to a 'hidden question': 'The hidden question behind my book is "What do these people enjoy?". The hidden question behind Dr Lewis's book is, "What do these people suffer from?" ' (Redfield 1960: 136).

Lewis also seemed to believe that they had studied the same village and that the differences between the results of their fieldwork were merely due to a difference in perspective. Such a difference undoubtedly existed. Lewis particularly did not want to present a 'neutral' picture of the village. Politically more committed than Redfield, he paid far more attention to what people suffered from. But did they really describe the same village, albeit from a different perspective and for a different purpose? There is room for doubt here. Redfield arrived in Tepoztlán just after the atrocities of the revolution, when the inhabitants had to flee from their village. Life in Tepoztlán was at the time of Redfield's fieldwork slowly returning to 'normal'. Between Redfield's stay there in 1926–7 and Lewis's fieldwork in 1943–4, Tepoztlán's population had grown rapidly. Lewis pays attention to the growth in population but gives little heed to its possible consequences. Many of the differences between Redfield's and Lewis's rendering of social relations can be explained in terms of population pressure resulting from rapid population growth (disappearance of communal land and communal labour, growing antagonism between landowners and landless people, distrust in inter-personal relations). I therefore think that Coy is largely right when he concludes:

> . . . that both accounts were legitimate in the context of the situation ruling at the two periods of time . . . at some time between 1929 and 1935 economic and demographic changes in Tepoztlán favoured the

> expression of different behaviour patterns from that of the exhausted survivors of the revolution.
>
> (Coy 1971: 56)

There is little doubt that Redfield misrepresented Tepoztlán to some extent but Lewis's account is biased too. Yet, the differences between the two accounts are also due to structural changes taking place during the intervening period of seventeen years.

There are also changes of a cyclical nature that may give rise to discrepancies. The disagreement between Mead (1949) and Fortune (1939) regarding the warlike habits of the New Guinea Arapesh seems related to a cyclical pattern of change. One should appreciate that the structure of many societies is influenced by cyclical processes, sometimes requiring cycles up to thirty or forty years. This holds true, for example, for those New Guinean societies in which herds of pigs are slowly built up to be collectively slaughtered in the context of huge socio-political rituals. Patterns of life before and after these dramatic events differ markedly. The same phenomenon can be seen in the different descriptions of another New Guinea society, the Tchambuli or Chambri (see Mead 1935 versus Gewertz 1983). In this case the 'facts' are not at stake; however, their interpretation is. Gewertz shows that if the Chambri men seemed absorbed in politics and ritual (in contrast with the more mundane involvements of the women), this was due not to some basic Tchambuli ethos, but to a response to circumstances, which freed the men from business-like behaviour so characteristic of the women and coincided with Mead's four months' visit.

Still, reviewing the ethnographic controversies, change as an explanation of disagreement does not play an important role. Span of time between original research and restudy is not very important because there is no simple relationship between change and time. Annette Weiner, studying the Trobrianders fifty years after Malinowski's pioneering research, notes that despite her famous predecessor's gloomy predictions about the future of Trobriand culture, much had remained unchanged (Weiner 1976: 25).

ERRORS OF OBSERVATION AND FRAUD

Fieldworkers do, of course, make mistakes and this would be the easiest way to dispense with ethnographic disagreements. The question of who is right and who is wrong arises especially where widely differing images of the 'same' society have been put forward. When in 1983, Freeman challenged virtually every statement ever made by Mead regarding Samoa, the one important single question seemed to be whose Samoa was the right one. There is little doubt that a number of Mead's statements were wrong (but so are several of Freeman's statements, who occasionally misquotes and ignores information running counter to his own argument!). In other cases of ethnographic controversy, too, there is a fairly simple answer. When Redfield painted his rosy picture of

Tepoztlán and ignored more than one hundred cases of crime reported to the police during his sojourn there, it is reasonable to call this an error (unless Redfield would have done so on purpose; in that case it would have been fraud).

Things become more complicated regarding differing definitions. When Goodenough (1956) and Fischer (1958), both having conducted strictly controlled quantitative surveys on Truk, in Micronesia, found they had arrived at substantially different views on such a seemingly unambiguous phenomenon as marital residence, they quickly concluded that they simply had used different definitions of matrilocality and patrilocality! Although differently defining concepts cannot be regarded as an error at all, the non-realization that different definitions are used often results in accusations of error.

Error borders on fraud. The accusation of fraud befell William F. Whyte. Boelen accused him of dabbling with facts. The famous account in which Whyte showed the relationship between ranking and performance, for instance, was according to Boelen not based on empirical fact (Boelen 1992: 30–1).

Ironically, however, in the few cases of probably deliberate (and known!) fraud that exist in ethnography there are very few factual differences between the fraudulent and the supposedly honest ethnography. A case in point is Donner's book containing her experiences with the Venezuelan Yanomamö. This book is, apart from fantasy, based on an account of a Venezuelan girl, Helena Valero, who had been kidnapped by the Yanomamö – and had lived with them for twenty-four years (Valero 1984). De Holmes, who unmasked the fraud, could find numerous stylistic parallels between Donner's account and the book in which Helena Valero's autobiography was published. This strongly suggested plagiarism. However, she could find only one, minor, ethnographic mistake (see Donner 1982; De Holmes 1983)!

Yet, in by far the majority of the controversial cases, errors and fraud are not that simple to ascertain. Instead, one has to conclude, once again, that the differences are due to divergences in research perspective.

DIFFERENCES IN RESEARCH PERSPECTIVE

Sociocultural systems of even small-scale, pre-industrial and pre-literate societies are complex. Although the ambition of anthropology, and of early ethnographic fieldworkers in particular, is to comprehend a society and its culture in its totality, no fieldworker is really able to cover this complex totality. This inability necessitates selection. Research invariably means looking at reality from a specific point of view. By far the majority of ethnographic discrepancies are due to rather implicit differences in research perspective. Several kinds of perspectives can be distinguished. I list three kinds of perspectives, not meaning to say that they exclude each other.

In the first place, one should remember that in anthropological fieldwork, the dominant instrument is a human individual. Human individuals differ in their outlook in terms of age, gender and personality, and these differences affect their ethnographic observations and their interpretations. The big difference between Malinowski and Weiner in their Trobriand fieldwork is that the former was a man, hailing from a patriarchical Central European culture (Poland), while the latter was an American woman, working at a time when modern feminism was gaining momentum. Whereas Malinowski kept aloof from a number of women's activities, regarding them as unimportant, Weiner became inexorably involved in them. She was literally dragged into a women's ceremony, and although 'I had little notion of what was being enacted, the great amount of time, energy, and emotion involved made me sense the importance of the event' (Weiner 1976: 7).

In the second place, we should not forget the more or less explicit political objectives of the scholar. Lewis with regard to Tepoztlán was quite explicit about his aims when he wrote:

> It seems to me that concern with what people suffer from is much more important than the study of enjoyment because it is more productive of insights about the human condition, about the dynamics of conflict and the forces of change.... To stress the enjoyment in peasant life (*as Redfield did, PK*) is to argue for its preservation.
>
> (Lewis 1961: 179)

Thirdly, one should realize that ethnographic facts are constructs whereby the theoretical orientations of the fieldworker are as important as the actual reality. And behind more or less explicit theoretical orientations, more implicit cultural assumptions held by the fieldworker colour his or her observations. Discussing the Zuñi controversy Bennett argued already in 1946 that what was needed was not so much an answer to the question of whose description was right and whose was wrong, but rather 'a reflexive analysis of the meanings of the respective interpretations' (Bennett 1946: 374). After all, reality does not dictate our description of it. It only responds to our way of asking questions. Some answers correspond to what was expected, others have to be rejected. According to this view knowledge is inevitably a product of a reality having an existence of its own – and a particular approach. Theoretical concepts and methods of observation cannot be seen as epistemologically neutral tools, but as tools responsible for the ways our perception of reality is cast (cf. Heisenberg 1969: 57). The most glaring ethnographic discrepancies seem to be related to differences in theoretical orientation. This poses the problem of comparison of theoretical orientations. In the next section of this chapter I shall concentrate on the issue of different theoretical orientations defining reality in a different way. By doing so I hope to go beyond the simplistic question of right or wrong.

METATHEORIZING

One or two remarks about reality and theory are in order here. Empirical research is based on the assumption that there is a reality outside the observer, or, at least, that there is a distinction between an observer and something being observed. The gap between observer and reality is bridged by our way of observing, our methodology if you wish, and therefore by already existing conceptions. These conceptions include reasons to study reality, implicit assumptions about the nature of reality, theories explaining reality, and so on. Some of these conceptions are quite explicit, but many of them are implicit. Theories belong to the first category, assumptions about reality to the second. For all their implicitness they still deeply influence the outcome of empirical research, such as ethnographic accounts.

Anthropology, as far as theorizing is concerned, has always been a divided house, containing theories that often appear to be incompatible or even incommensurable. Still, there have been periods when anthropology came close to Kuhn's normal science, in which recognized scientific achievements 'served for a time implicitly to define the legitimate problems and methods of a research field for succeeding generations of practitioners' (Kuhn 1970: 10). In the 1960s such a relatively homogeneous period came to an end when structural-functionalism was replaced by a medley of alternative approaches. Because at the same time the volume of ethnographic research rose dramatically many of the restudies and the ethnographic discrepancies belong to the 1970s and later, and therefore to a theoretically very different and in itself heterogeneous era.

To handle ethnographic accounts that differ or even conflict in terms of theoretical background one must find a way to handle theoretical differentiation. For convenience, I use a simple concept of what a theory is: a set of interrelated propositions forming some sort of a logical system and accounting for a specified part of reality. This brings theoretical differences down to differences in propositions. Anthropological theories differ from each other in many respects, not in just one. After all, a theory is a multi-dimensional phenomenon.

The differences between theoretical propositions are often expressed in terms of oppositions. One explanation of this is that new approaches are often conceived in direct contradistinction to predecessors. But theories are often also logically each other's opposites. Barrett (1984) lists some forty sets of propositional differences but this number is misleading. His list is not exhaustive, and furthermore, many of the so-called differences overlap.

Dealing with these differences requires an anthropological meta-theory – a systematic study of the nature and structure of anthropological theories or a theory of theories. Unlike in sociology (see Ritzer 1992) metatheorizing is not yet a genre in anthropological writing. For that matter, even theorizing is hardly a genre in a discipline that stresses ethnography (ironically it is precisely ethnography that forces us to become metatheoreticians!). Other disciplines, such as physics, can in this respect provide a source of inspiration. In 1973 the physicist Holton argued that the history of his discipline could be described in terms of a limited number of themes and their opposites, or anti-themes (Holton 1973). For example:

- experience versus logical formalism
- complexity versus simplicity
- reductionism versus holism
- discontinuity versus continuity
- mechanistic versus teleological explanations.

According to Holton, theories may be seen as specific combinations of such themes and anti-themes. This seems to be true for anthropology as well: there is a limited number of differences between theories that together cover the characteristics of theoretical and methodological alternatives. These differences are often described in terms of oppositions and may even be called *binary oppositions* (to borrow a concept from structuralist anthropology). A binary opposition consists of a set of two terms that exclude each other from a certain point of view, and therefore can be understood only in relation to each other. On the other hand, differences may quite unwarrantedly be conceived of as an opposition or a contradiction. In any case, every set of related terms logically implies a third term of a higher order. For convenience's sake I call these third terms *dimensions*. Many polemics lack clarity in this respect and often are monologues dealing with entirely different subjects rather than dialogues in which the discussants contribute to each other's views. The discussants may use the same terms, but fail to make clear that they belong to very different discourses.

Therefore, the first question is what are the main types of features, dimensions or third terms of anthropological theories? The second question is what are the differences per dimension when looking at the various theories held at the moment? The longer lists, such as Barrett's, can be reduced to a brief list of eight strategic dimensions of anthropological theory. I list these eight dimensions, including one or more sets of opposed terms currently used to indicate contrasting points of view (this inventory of sets is not meant to be complete; I also refrain from assessing the sets – I use them as I found them in the literature):

1 the nature of scientific statements:
    nomothetic versus idiographic
    explanation versus description
    cause versus purpose
    explanation versus understanding
2 the nature of the categories used:
    emic versus etic

phenomenological versus positivist
qualitative versus quantitative

3 the nature of social relations:
    harmonious versus conflicting
    consensus versus conflict

4 the nature of the relationship between individual and society:
    actionist versus system dominated
    agency versus structure
    event versus structure
    content versus form
    motive versus function

5 the locus of explanations:
    matter versus mind
    materialism versus idealism
    reductionism versus holism

6 the dimension of time:
    synchronic versus diachronic
    static versus dynamic
    anthropology versus history

7 the use made of knowledge:
    for *status quo* versus emancipatory
    science versus politics
    pure versus applied

8 the origins of sociocultural change:
    exogenous versus endogenous
    diffusion versus evolution.

The recent history of theory in anthropology shows fierce polemics over these differences. Because of the origins of new theoretical perspectives and the need to defend the new ones from the established ones the differences often became incompatible opposites. *Socio*-logically understandable, this is *logically* not necessary.

From a logical point of view there are basically two ways of dealing with opposing terms: one chooses for one term, thereby rejecting the other; or one tries to overcome the opposition, accepting the necessary relationship between the terms. Those who choose the first way follow the well-trodden path that is characteristically European in its approach to dualism. This approach can be characterized as thinking in terms of dichotomies: it is 'either-or' thinking (the dialectical tradition is an obvious exception to dichotomic thinking). One ethnographic account is right, the other is, consequently and inevitably wrong. To go beyond these simple and simplistic dichotomies requires a closer and more detached scrutiny of the dimensions and the nature of the relationship between the opposed terms, thus bringing us to the question of commensurability.

Regarding the first dimension, the nature of statements, one must admit that the terms 'nomothetic' and 'idiographic' are indeed basically different, but that, on the other hand, they pre-suppose each other. One cannot arrive at reliable nomothetic statements without idiographic ones, and idiographic statements, or statements of fact, are invariably cast in nomothetic terms – at least, as soon as they are scientifically interesting. Because the dimension is, with regard to ethnographic discrepancies, not very important – ethnography by its very nature tends to be idiographic – I will not go further than this.

The terms 'etic' and 'emic' pose a different problem. Emic terms are those that are recognized as meaningful by bearers of a culture, as members of a specific society. Etic terms are the ones regarded as useful by members of the scientific community. Apparently clear-cut, the distinction offers problems, if only because the so-called 'etic' terms are predominantly derived from European languages, and embedded in Western cultures. It has been shown in a number of cases that several scientific terms are Western emic, rather than etic, ones. This certainly applies to many anthropological terms (although one should add here that a number of anthropological concepts, like 'tabu', 'totem', 'potlatch', and 'Big Man', originate from non-Western societies, which does not make them less cultural or emic, of course). Scientific concepts are not reducible to sense perceptions, as the early logical-positivists hoped, and are invariably cultural constructs. Again, in the present context this dimension is not very important.

The third dimension of harmony and conflict runs through Western thinking as a continuous thread, some theorists taking conflict as their basic metaphor (for example, Marxism), others harmony, or, less abstract, the biological organism (for example, structural-functionalism). However, nowadays it is generally recognized that a view purely in terms of conflict is as unrealistic as its opposite. The question is how in a given sociocultural situation the two relate to each other.

The fourth dimension too shows a rapprochement. The issue of the relationship between individual and society is a perennial element in Western thinking, not only in the social sciences where it was systematically investigated for the first time by Durkheim, but also in history. In history the often-raised question was whether Great Men made History, or whether History made Great Men. The classical way out of this dilemma is of course Marx's famous statement in *The Eighteenth Brumaire of Louis Bonaparte* (1852), where he states that 'people make their own history, but they do not make it from their own free will, under conditions chosen by themselves, but under given and transmitted circumstances, encountered straight away'.

This insight notwithstanding, social scientific views have shuttled back and forth between extreme system-oriented approaches, such as structural-functionalism, and equally extreme individual-oriented or actor-oriented approaches, such as transactionalism.

In recent years extremes have become rare. What seems to dominate at present is rather the search for a view that transcends the extremes. Examples are the work of Giddens, who parenthetically explicitly takes Marx's just quoted statement as one of his points of departure (Giddens 1984: xxi), of Bourdieu and his theory of praxis, again explicitly trying to transcend false oppositions (Bourdieu 1977), and several others.

There are a few discrepancies that are based on the false opposition between actor- and system-oriented approach, or rather where a system-oriented approach has been criticized from an actor-oriented approach. One of them concerns Evans-Pritchard's famous study *The Nuer* (1940), an account that comes close to being an exemplar in the Kuhnian sense of the term for structural-functionalist research. Boissevain (1974) pointed out that the meagre data offered by Evans-Pritchard on the actual behaviour of the Nuer contradict the abstract model presented. Apparently the Nuer do not always allow themselves to be guided by the abstract models said to characterize their society. There are also examples of ethnographic accounts stressing individualism that have been shown to be incorrect – for instance, Barth's study of the Swat Pathans (1969). Asad (1972), using Barth's own empirical data, demonstrates that the latter severely underestimates the structural constraints that obtain in Swat Pathan. Asad convincingly argues that in Swat Pathan leaders, as well as followers, are far less free in exercising choice than Barth wants his readers to believe and that there are structures in Swat Pathan which, in a Durkheimian sense, channel the behaviour of purportedly free individuals.

The fifth opposition is equally basic of Western thinking: Is the Archimedean locus of explanation of sociocultural phenomena situated in the mind or in matter? There are various twin-terms in use to designate this opposition – idealism versus materialism for instance – but these are by no means the only ones. In recent anthropology the main opposition between theories that may be seen in terms of a mind–matter opposition is the one between structuralism and (cultural) materialism. Apart from general polemics between advocates of both views, there are many examples of conflicting ethnographic accounts where the differences follow from this difference in mode of explanation. The example referred to at the beginning of this chapter is only one case. See also Lévi-Strauss versus Aspelin (Aspelin 1976) and Beck versus Den Ouden (Beck 1970; Den Ouden 1975).

The sixth opposition was once quite strong, especially in British social anthropology. Due to the renewed opening in the direction of history, however, it has lost its character of either/or opposition: fieldworkers have come to realize that what is ethnographically present at a certain moment is but a phase in an ongoing temporal process. An increasing number of ethnographies bear testimony of this insight.

The seventh opposition is present in discussions about ethnographic disagreements, but far less than its nature would lead one to assume. It touches the political meaning of ethnographic research, the use made of ethnography but also the issue of the origins of research questions. The opposition has different designations or meanings. A number of scholars let their scientific interests be guided by their perceptions of the interests of the people among whom they work. Others say that their primary interest is what Wright Mills once called 'the politics of truth'. They shy away from direct political involvement, arguing that scientific researchers should not be involved in politics. To me this is an untenable position, for several reasons. One is that, as far as ethnographic knowledge can be used, those in power have more access to it than others. Another is that the nature of knowledge was and is more geared to colonial and post-colonial interests than to the interest of those whose ways of life have been studied. For those reasons I prefer the terms '*status quo*' and 'emancipatory'. An important question is who judges the ethnography's resemblance to reality: the community of observers, or the community of the observed?

There are few known examples of discrepancies going back to this difference (the Redfield–Lewis controversy is one, however). The reason is that in but a very small number of the published ethnographies do we know anything at all of the judgement of the observed! It is my conviction that if research problems had been formulated by the observed, the majority of ethnographic accounts would be very different. And that if ethnographic accounts were systematically reviewed by those concerned, many disagreements about how to perceive reality would surface.

Finally, the eighth dimension, though a source of debate one or two generations ago, is momentarily not a serious issue. Nobody seriously doubts that processes of continuity and change are invariably the outcome of an intricate concatenation of internal and external factors. And I know of no major case of ethnographic disagreement revolving around this distinction.

BEYOND THE EITHER/OR CHOICE OF RIGHT OR WRONG

As I argued earlier, the main reason why ethnographers disagree is that their theoretical orientations differ. As a result, the way they look at reality also differs. And above, I argued that as far as theoretical orientations are concerned the two differences, especially relevant in this context, are found in the domain of explanation and in the political meaning of scientific research. Other oppositions either play no significant role in ethnographic disagreements, or are at the moment being actively resolved.

The challenge is to go beyond the age-old opposition of mind and matter, and of political neutrality and partisanship. It is truly a challenge because there is more involved than theory *strictu sensu*. In the social sciences theories are not only instruments to explain reality. They are also expressions of existential circumstances of their authors, to put it kindly, or ill-disguised particularistic ideologies – to put it less kindly. The conditions to go beyond old oppositions are favourable, however. Ethnography is increasingly becoming a collective affair, with several scholars working in the same field. 'There are no more isolated pioneers, no Malinowskian monarchs of all they once surveyed' wrote Kuper recently (Kuper 1992: 68). Fardon (1990) calls this phenomenon 'regionalization' or 'localizing' of fieldwork. Collaboration of anthropologists working in the same area is likely to have a double effect: it will bring about better ethnography (because others may be looking over your shoulder and, in any case, know first-hand what you are talking about), and it will bring about theoretical clarity (because others are looking at the same phenomena albeit from a different perspective).

This project, however different from the ethnographic project that characterized anthropology in its early years is no less important: as I argued above, ethnographic specificity is not disappearing. On the contrary, in Asia, Africa but also in Europe it is gaining strength. As constructs, ethnic identities are contested, and so are the contributions of scholars (cf. Kloos 1995; McDonald 1987; Peletz 1993). Still, theoretical rigour and a method of handling ethnographic discrepancies remain the most important contributions anthropology has to offer.

ACKNOWLEDGEMENTS

I am indebted to an unknown referee and to Susan Caolo Boot for improving my use of a language not my own.

REFERENCES

Ahlbrinck, W. G. (1931) *Encyclopaedie der Karaiben*, Amsterdam: Koninklijke Akademie van Wetenschappen.

Asad, T. (1972) 'Market model, class structure and consent. A reconsideration of Swat political organization', *Man* 7: 74–94.

Aspelin, P. L. (1976) 'Nambicuara economic dualism: Lévi-Strauss in the garden once again', *Bijdragen Taal-, Land-en Volkenkunde* 132: 1–31.

—— (1978) 'Comments', *Bijdragen Taal-, Land-en Volkenkunde* 134: 158–61.

—— (1979) 'The ethnography of Nambicuara agriculture', *Bijdragen Taal-, Land-en Volkenkunde* 135: 18–58.

Barrett, S. R. (1984) *The Rebirth of Anthropological Theory*, Toronto: University of Toronto Press.

Barth, F. (1969) *Political Leadership among Swat Pathans*, London: The Athlone Press.

Bateson, C. (1984) *With a Daughter's Eye. A Memoir of Margaret Mead and Gregory Bateson*, New York: Simon & Schuster.

Beck, B. E. F. (1970) 'The right–left division of South Indian society', *Journal of Asian Studies* 29, 4: 779–98.

—— (1972) *Peasant Society in Konku. A Study of Right and Left Subcastes in South India*, Vancouver: University of British Columbia Press.

Bennett, J. W. (1946) 'The interpretation of Pueblo culture: a question of values', *Southwestern Journal of Anthropology* 2: 361–74.

Boelen, W. A. M. (1992) 'Cornerville revisited', *Journal of Contemporary Ethnography* 21(1): 11–51.

Boissevain, J. (1974) *Friends of Friends. Networks, Manipulators and Coalitions*, Oxford: Basil Blackwell.

Bourdieu, P. (1977) *Outline of a Theory of Practice*, Cambridge: Cambridge University Press.

Bovenkerk, F. (1992) 'Street Corner Society: een geval van wetenschappelijke fraude?' in H. Moerland et al. (eds), *De menselijke maat. Opstellen ter gelegenheid van het afscheid van Prof dr G. P. Hoefnagels*, Arnhem: Gouda Quint, 285–304.

Coy, P. (1971) 'A watershed in Mexican rural history: some thoughts on the reconciliation of conflicting interpretations', *Journal of Latin American Studies* 3: 39–57.

De Holmes, R. B. (1983) 'Shabono: scandal of superb social science?', *American Anthropologist* 85: 664–7.

Donner, F. (1982) *Shabono. A Visit to a Remote and Magical World in the Heart of the South American Jungle*, New York: Delacorte.

Evans-Pritchard, E. E. (1940) *The Nuer: A Description of the Modes of Livelihood and Political Institutions of a Nilotic People*, Oxford: Clarendon Press.

Fardon, R. (ed.) (1990) *Localizing Strategies. Regional Traditions in Ethnographic Writing*, Edinburgh/Washington: Scottish Academic Press/Smithsonian Institution Press.

Fischer, J. L. (1958) 'The classification of residence rules', *American Anthropologist* 60: 508–17.

Fortune, R. (1939) 'Arapesh warfare', *American Anthropologist* 41: 22–41.

Freeman, D. (1983) *Margaret Mead and Samoa. The Making and Unmaking of an Anthropological Myth*, Cambridge MA: Harvard University Press.

Gewertz, D. B. (1983) *Sepik River Societies: A Historical Ethnography of the Chambri and Their Neighbors*, New Haven: Yale University Press.

Giddens, A. (1984) *The Constitution of Society. Outline of the Theory of Structuration*, Cambridge: Polity Press.

Goodenough, W. H. (1956) 'Residence rules', *Southwestern Journal of Anthropology* 12: 22–37.

Harris, M. (1968) *The Rise of Anthropological Theory*, London: Routledge & Kegan Paul.

Heider, K. (1988) 'The Rashomon effect: when ethnographers disagree', *American Anthropologist* 90(1): 73–81.

Heisenberg, W. (1969) *Physics and Philosophy. The Revolution in Modern Science*, London: George Allen & Unwin.

Holmes, L. D. (1957) *The Restudy of Manu'an Culture. A Problem in Methodology*, Northwestern University Ph.D. thesis: Ann Arbor Microfilms No. 23.514.

—— (1983) 'A tale of two studies', *American Anthropologist* 85: 929–35.

—— (1987) *Quest for the Real Samoa. The Mead/Freeman Controversy and Beyond*. South Hadley MA: Bergin and Garvey.

Holton, G. (1973) *Thematic Origins of Scientific Thought. Kepler to Einstein*, Cambridge MA: MIT Press.

Kloos, P. (1968) 'Becoming a Pïyei: variability and similarity in Carib shamanism', *Antropologica* (Caracas) 24: 3–25.

—— (1971) *The Maroni River Caribs of Surinam*, Assen: Van Gorcum.

—— (1988a) *Door het oog van de antropoloog. Botsende visies bij heronderzoek*, Muiderberg: D. Coutinho.

—— (1988b) 'No knowledge without a knowing subject' in R.G. Burgess (ed.), *Qualitative Methodology: A Research Annual*, Volume I: *Conducting Qualitative Research*, Greenwich CT: Jai Press, 221–41.

—— (1993) 'Globalization, localization, and violence', *Folk* 35: 5–16.

—— (1994) 'Replication, restudy, and the nature of anthropological fieldwork' in R. van der Veer, M. IJzendoorn and J. Valsiner (eds), *Reconstructing the Mind:*

Replicability in Research on Human Development, Norwood: Ablex Publishing Corporation, 37–56.

—— (1995) 'Publish and perish. Nationalism and social research in Sri Lanka', *Social Anthropology* 3(2): 115–28.

Kuhn, T. S. (1970) *The Structure of Scientific Revolutions*, Chicago: University of Chicago Press.

Kuper, A. (1992) 'Post-modernism and the Great Kalahari debate', *Social Anthropology* 1: 57–71.

Leach, E. R. (1984) 'Glimpses of the unmentionable in the history of British social anthropology', *Annual Review of Anthropology* 13: 1–23.

—— (1989) 'Writing anthropology', *American Ethnologist* 16(1): 137–41.

Lévi-Strauss, C. (1955) *Tristes Tropiques*, Paris: Plon.

—— (1963) *Structural Anthropology*, New York: Basic Books.

Lewis, O. (1951) *Life in a Mexican Village: Tepoztlán Restudied*, Champaign: University of Illinois Press.

—— (1961) 'Some of my best friends are peasants', *Human Organization* 19(4): 179–80.

Li An-Che (1937) 'Zuñi: Some observations and queries', *American Anthropologist* 39: 62–76.

McDonald, M. (1987) 'The politics of fieldwork in Brittany' in Anthony Jackson (ed.), *Anthropology at Home*, London: Tavistock Publications, 120–38.

Magaña, E. (1988) *Orión y la mujer Pléyades. Simbolismo astronómico de los indios kaliña de Surinam*, Amsterdam: CEDLA.

Marx, K. (1852) 'Der 18te Brumaire des Louis Napoleon', in K. Marx and F. Engels (1978) *Werke*, Band 8, Berlin: Dietz Verlag, 111–207.

Mead, M. (1928) *Coming of Age in Samoa*, New York: William Morrow.

—— (1930) *Social Organization of Manu'a*, Honolulu: Bernice P. Bishop Museum bulletin.

—— (1935) *Sex and Temperament in Three Primitive Societies*, New York: William Morrow.

—— (1949) 'The Mountain Arapesh', *Anthropological Papers of the American Museum of Natural History* 41 (3).

Ouden, J. H. B. den (1975) *De onaanraakbaren van Konkunad. Een onderzoek naar veranderingen in de sociale positie van de Scheduled Castes in een dorp van het district Coimbatore, India*, Wageningen: H.Veenman.

—— (1977) *De onaanraakbaren van Konkunad. Een onderzoek naar de positieverandering van de Scheduled Castes in een dorp van het district Coimbatore, India* (Deel II), Wageningen: Vakgroep Agrarische Sociologie van de niet-westerse gebieden.

Peletz, M. G. (1993) 'Sacred texts and dangerous words: the politics of law and cultural rationalization in Malaysia', *Comparative Studies in Society and History* 35(1): 66–109.

Redfield, R. (1930) *Tepoztlán: A Mexican Village*, Chicago: University of Chicago Press.

—— (1960) *The Little Community and Peasant Society and Culture*, Chicago: University of Chicago Press.

Ritzer, G. (ed.) (1992) *Metatheorizing*, London: Sage Publications.

Stocking, G. W. (ed.) (1983) *Observers Observed. Essays on Ethnographic Fieldwork*, History of Anthropology, Vol. 1, Wisconsin: The University of Wisconsin Press.

Valero, H. (1984) *Yo soy Napëyoma. Relato de una mujer raptada por los indígenas Yanomami*, Caracas: Fundacíon la Salla de Ciencias Naturales.

Weiner, A. B. (1976) *Women of Value, Men of Renown. New Perspectives in Trobriand Exchange*, Austin: University of Texas Press.

Whyte, W. F. (1943) *Street Corner Society. The Social Structure of an Italian Slum*, Chicago: University of Chicago Press.

5

NATION AND DEMOCRACY

Conflict or Balance?

Jan P. Verhoogt

Since World War II Dutch politicians have spent much energy on building up a welfare state in their country. During the late 1950s and 1960s a generous social security system was developed on the basis of an expanding market economy. This system brought about far-reaching social equality or social democracy. During the 1970s the emphasis in Dutch politics was on enlarging opportunities for effective citizen participation on various levels of collective decision-making in social and political life. Government facilities were provided to reach this aim. This policy resulted in a substantial extension of political equality or political democracy in this country. The Dutch welfare state acquired some reputation in Western society as a proper manifestation of the universal principles of social and political democracy.

Although during recent decades a large majority of the Dutch people have voted for the political parties which have built up the welfare state, that is not to say that they are really satisfied with the policy of their government. For, at the same time, an increasing number of citizens are of the opinion that normal life is undermined by a variety of problems for which they also hold these parties responsible – increasing drug abuse and the various kinds of criminality it involves, changes in public lifestyle in the city districts as a result of the entrance of large groups of immigrants, etc. Growing discontent in the population was indicated by a recent poll held by a research institute of the government. The results made it clear that a large majority of the population considers the growth and influence of ethnic minorities by far the greatest problem in Dutch society and this, in their view, is not taken seriously enough by official politics.

Using nationalist and anti-democratic slogans, leaders of a militant right-wing party try to direct these feelings of discontent in the population against minority groups in society, as well as against the dominant political parties. The leaders of this party claim that while the government parties were focused on building up the welfare state, at the same time they were seriously neglecting the common values and inherited way of life of the Dutch people. Although this right-wing party is still relatively small, the results of the poll mentioned above indicate that a latent breeding ground does exist for nationalist and anti-democratic reactions among a large section of the Dutch people.

We may conclude that Dutch social and political life is torn by a fundamental and somewhat paradoxical conflict. In terms of voting behaviour the decision-making process meant to built up the welfare state is supported by a large majority of the population. At the same time, however, the welfare state and its policy is a source of collective discontent and frustration which even arouses latent sympathy to nationalist and anti-democratic slogans. It should be recognized that such tendencies could suddenly and unexpectedly turn into a manifest and active political force that might then really endanger democracy.

How can we explain the conflicting political orientations which the Dutch welfare state actually arouses? The welfare state was built up by Liberal, Social Democratic and Christian Democratic parties working together in changing coalitions. How did the founding fathers of the political theories of the Enlightenment, from which these parties originally arose, understand the unity and identity of national communities while they elaborated their classic concepts of democracy? Did the political leaders who built up the welfare state neglect more balanced views on this point held by their founding fathers? Finding an answer to these questions is the main subject of this chapter. It may further a better understanding of the conflict which tears social and political life apart and help us to deal with the problem in daily political life.

In the history of political theory in line with the Enlightenment view two dominant positions can be observed: Locke's liberal theory on the one hand, and Rousseau's radical theory which deeply influenced Marx and Marxism on the other. What views on democracy and national community are implied in those classic political theories? It should be noticed that Locke and Rousseau reacted to and were influenced by the political and religious situation in the countries in which they were living. Therefore we will start this chapter with a short analysis of the origin and nature of the classic European nation-state with special attention to England and France. After that we will look at the meaning of the concepts of democracy and national community in the theories of Locke and Rousseau. Then, we shall describe how these concepts were redefined during the second half of the nineteenth century. Next, we will focus on the influence of the Enlightenment political ideas described above on the social and political history of the Dutch nation-state, in which Christian Democratic parties also played a substantial role. Finally, we will make a few general remarks on the relationship between nation and democracy in our time.

THE ORIGIN AND NATURE OF THE EUROPEAN NATION-STATE

In his classic discussion of the idea of sovereignty, Hinsley explains that in early human history the State, as a structure of command, imposed itself on the community. Although he considers the establishment of the State an important condition for sovereignty, Hinsley points to a second condition to be fulfilled. The idea of sovereignty also entails that people identify to some extent the claims of the State with the needs of their community. 'It is only when the community responds to the State and the State responds to the community in which it rules that the discussion of political power can take place in terms of sovereignty' (Hinsley 1989: 16ff.).

Hinsley's general idea about sovereignty can be specified with respect to the foundation of the classic nation-states in Europe after the Reformation. On the one hand, church leaders, Protestant as well as Roman Catholic, were of the opinion that what they claimed to be the true doctrine should be defended by the State. On the other hand, kings and princes realized that unity of religion was a necessary condition for the maintenance of law and order in their territories. 'The belief was general on the side of churchmen that pure doctrine ought to be maintained by public authority, and on the side of the statesmen that unity of religion was an indispensable condition of public order' (Sabine and Thorson 1973: 333).

Although they had different points of departure, church leaders and worldly men of power together became responsible for the strong mingling of State and Christian religion in Europe at that time. As a matter of fact, this close connection between State and religion gave rise to violent suppression and wars. Within state territories, defenders of what was considered to be the false doctrine were persecuted. Besides that, wars were carried on between states which had declared that what they saw as the true doctrine was to be the official state religion. It can be argued that these religious conflicts and wars laid the foundations of England as a Protestant nation-state and France as a Roman Catholic nation-state. In both countries the absolute monarchy symbolized and defended the specific Christian doctrine which founded the unity and identity of their nation (Sabine and Thorson 1973: 334).

The lasting violence and wars which resulted from the intermingling of State and Christian doctrines gave rise to the broad movement of Humanism and Enlightenment that spread over Europe during the sixteenth and seventeenth centuries. It was claimed by the leaders of this movement that war and violence could only be brought to an end when the State dissociated itself from Christian doctrines and used its power and authority on behalf of universal principles of justice based on human rights and democracy. However in this political philosophy of the Enlightenment view, a difficult theoretical question with far-reaching practical consequences was implied. For it soon appeared that rational and universal principles of democracy and human rights were not in themselves a sufficient basis to found a stable and unified society. Locke and Rousseau, the founding fathers of the political philosophy of the Enlightenment, recognized this problem but found very different solutions for it.

LOCKE'S CONCEPTION OF POLITICAL DEMOCRACY

Locke disagreed with his liberal friends who were convinced that in England the protection of human rights was guaranteed by the 'Ancient Constitution'. In his opinion customs and traditions are inherently conservative and arbitrary. Only reason could found a truly obligatory and universal theory on state and human rights that may suppose 'tacit consent' of every right thinking human being (Resnick 1984: 102).

Locke's main thesis implies that protection of basic rights on 'life, liberty and estate', summed up in the basic right to property, is the primary reason for existence of the State (Locke 1690: VII). With this argument he turned against the connection between the English government and the Roman Catholic church in his day. According to Locke the State's only concern with religious affairs should consist in the protection of the right to property, which in his view also implied the right to property of one's own religious conviction. Thus Locke's view on the right to property formally justified religious tolerance (Sabine and Thorson 1973: 496). Although Locke adjudged a crucial role to the government in enforcing basic rights, he also realized that citizens need to be protected against governmental authorities with more ambitions than exercising their primary task. In Locke's view this aim could only be reached when the governors were controlled by those who were governed. For this reason Locke articulated his concept of basic human rights in terms of the basic principles of political democracy which in his view should be primarily built on the general franchise. 'Von der Logik seiner Argumentation aus . . . könnte nur auf ein allgemeines und gleiches Wahlrecht für alle Bürger geschlossen werden' (Brocker 1991: 58).

However, Locke's conception of the State enforcing basic human rights, summed up in the right to property, is only half the story of his political philosophy. Dubiel has pointed out that Locke came to the view that a state could only fulfil its primary task in a society held together by a collective feeling of solidarity and a structure of norms and institutions which already entailed a notion of justice, a sense of mine and thine, etc. (Dubiel 1990: 126). Locke was convinced that this condition was actually fulfilled in his native country. The crucial role his country played in his political theory becomes more explicit in Locke's criticism of slavery in which he explains that slavery not only violates human rights but is contrary to the identity of the English nation as well (Farr 1986: 269). Besides that, the theological presuppositions of his political theory, together with his personal involvement in the Protestant conspiracy, indicate Locke's deep conviction that the traditional identity of the English nation had always been and should remain Protestant (Sap 1993: 192ff.).

We may conclude that when Locke once appealed to his countrymen for 'explicit consent' with their nation because of its high standards of liberalism, the norms and institutions based in Protestantism which kept the English nation-state as a moral community together were in fact included in those standards. So in Locke's liberal philosophy universal and abstract principles of basic rights and democracy were closely connected with the historical idea of a national community based on Christian norms and institutions. It should be recognized, however, that as a liberal theorist Locke had no intrinsic connection with this idea; he understood the specific unity and identity of his national community primarily in functional terms as a favourable condition for the spread of his liberal political ideas (Zvesper 1984: 60).

ROUSSEAU'S CONCEPTION OF RADICAL DEMOCRACY

Rousseau sharply criticized daily life in the higher circles in a big city like Paris, where he lived during his formative years. Competition of interests, jealousy and a permanent inclination to deceit were their main incentives. Rousseau was convinced that this attitude to life was already penetrating into French society as a whole and would undermine its moral integration and harmony (Oerlemans 1988: 135ff.).

Contrary to this, Rousseau developed the idea of an alternative society based on the principle of radical democracy. This principle firstly implied that political democracy as a mechanism for making collective decisions should not only be applied on the level of society as a whole, but in its various subgroups as well. Besides that, Rousseau emphasized that political democracy presupposes for its functioning a large measure of social equality or social democracy. Rousseau held the view that only radical democracy would provide the necessary conditions for human emancipation and development.

At this point the difference between Rousseau and Locke should be recognized. While in Locke's liberal political theory a connection with the English Protestant nation-state was maintained, Rousseau radically broke with the French nation-state as a social and moral unity founded in Roman Catholicism. But what, then, holds Rousseau's alternative society together?

In the first instance Rousseau held the somewhat romantic idea that radical democracy all by itself would give rise to social unity and harmony. This idea, however, is contrary to the rather strongly oppressive implications of his concept of democracy. For Rousseau had explained that if the 'volonté générale' couldn't be reached by discussion, decisions had to be made by majority vote, which had to be unconditionally accepted by minority groups (Rousseau 1762: III). Riley pointed out the repressive implications of Rousseau's concept of radical democracy. It forces people to accept that one's own freedom comes to full advantage only in doing the general will of the community, which implies a real 'denaturing' of their natural passions (Riley 1991: 59).

Just because of its oppressive implications, Rousseau's concept of radical democracy had to be supplemented by a strong principle of solidarity and social cohesion. Rousseau elaborated this condition in terms of a civil religion, described by Dubiel as the dynamic force of social integration which kept civil society together (Dubiel 1990: 127). The practice of civil religion holds that the political authorities in radical democracies should consciously try to raise feelings of national unity and solidarity with the citizens by means of education, propaganda, etc. It should be emphasized that the feelings thus raised involve no universal sentiments of common brotherhood; rather they are feelings of patriotism and loyalty to one's national community: 'these patriotic emotions depend for their force on their exclusiveness'. Rousseau even considered nationalism as the mother of all virtues (Keohane 1978: 480).

We may conclude that Locke, as well as Rousseau, built on the Enlightenment concept of justice which they articulated in some basic principles of democracy. They also recognized, however, that democracy could only survive when it is based on historically defined national communities as social and moral entities. So from maintaining a balanced relationship between abstract principles of democracy and nation as a historically defined community is a basic point of departure of the founding fathers of Enlightenment political philosophy. As Locke and Rousseau articulated the abstract principles of democracy in different directions, they also held different ideas about the nature of the community on which democracy should be built. Locke related his concept of political democracy to the English nation-state held together by Christian norms and institutions. In the name of radical democracy, Rousseau, in the first instance, broke with the French nation-state dominated by the Roman Catholic church. In the alternative radical democratic society, political leaders should use effective methods to arouse again nationalistic sentiments of solidarity and togetherness. Locke's concept of democracy, as well as Rousseau's, strongly influenced the political history of eighteenth-century Europe and America.

THE MODERNIZATION OF THE NATION-STATE

'The basic characteristic of the modern nation and everything connected with it is its modernity.' Hobsbawm (1990: 18) explains this somewhat circular statement by emphasizing that the modern nation is closely connected with modern phenomena like democracy and mass participation. In line with this idea Hobsbawm localizes the origin of the modern nation-state in the American and French Revolutions because in his eyes both revolutions were basically people's movements.

I think Hobsbawm's statement needs some qualification. Defining the modern nation exclusively in terms of the abstract principles of democracy makes it very difficult to do justice to the specific unity and identity which still characterize classic nation-states like England and France and many other nations which arose in the history of Europe. For that reason we preferred to turn the explanation around. In the foregoing we took our point of departure in the early history of these nation-states when their specific unity and identity were founded in traditional norms and institutions, symbolized and defended by absolute monarchies. In the course of European history, these nation-states then came under pressure from revolutionary movements which were inspired by the abstract and universal Enlightenment principles of basic rights and democracy. As these principles were elaborated by Locke and Rousseau in rather different concepts of democracy, this also explains the difference between the American and French Revolutions which arose from these concepts.

The American Revolution became the source of inspiration for the various liberal movements that spread across Europe during the first half of the nineteenth century. These movements aimed at restriction of the power and influence of established authoritarian regimes in their countries by introducing some kind of constitution that guaranteed basic rights and political democracy. So these movements focused primarily on the political democratization of national state-powers while, at the same time, they largely respected the integrity of national communities kept together by traditional norms and institutions, which is in line with the basic ideas of Locke described above.

Although it arose from a spirit of liberalism, the French Revolution soon came under the spell of the radical ideas of Rousseau. From that moment on this revolutionary movement violently turned against the facts and symbols of the *ancien régime*, which clearly indicates its hostility to national communities kept together by traditional norms and institutions. However, consistent with the ideas of Rousseau as well, within a decade this radical democratic movement had changed into a radical nationalist movement under the command of the Jacobins, who forcefully executed the slogan that the nation is 'one and indivisible'.

The social and political history of Europe and America during the second half of the nineteenth century was deeply influenced by the facts and promises of progress of the Industrial Revolution. Its fabulous technology was derived from the successful natural sciences, which then also inspired the rise of positivist sciences on man and society. In line with these developments in science and society, the basic concepts of democracy as founded by Locke and Rousseau were redefined in nineteenth-century political philosophy in terms of psychological and materialistic needs. As a result these concepts were separated from any connection with historically defined moral and social communities as implied in the philosophies of Locke and Rousseau.

Thus Locke's liberal ideas were redefined by Bentham in terms of psychological utilitarianism which explains human behaviour from the drive of 'seeking pleasure and avoiding pain'. From this perspective, political democracy and the market mechanism derived their final meaning from their contributions to collective welfare, described as 'the greatest happiness to the greatest numbers'. It should be noticed that liberalism's growing interest at that time in a more active State was also justified on utilitarian grounds, 'for it provided a defence of selective electorally controlled state intervention to help maximize the public good' (Held 1987: 92ff.).

Contrary to the utilitarian vision of human history as continuous progress, Marx understood nineteenth-century industrial society in terms of a growing gap between the poor and the rich. This brought him to elaborating Rousseau's ideas into a radical criticism of the capitalist mode of production, which also implied a criticism of nationalism and Christianity because, in Marx's view, these ideologies legitimized this repressive mode of production. Marx was convinced that capitalism would collapse because in the end it would raise the international proletarian class as its revolutionary counter-force. He held the view that only in a classless society could the ideas of collective wealth and radical democracy which Rousseau had in mind be realized. It should be noted that Marx's thoughts gave rise to a variety of Marxisms – on the one hand, to revolutionary communist movements which forcefully overthrew national communities kept together by traditional norms and institutions, and also to social democratic parties which used the framework of liberal democracy in historical nation-states to reach Marx's aims (Held 1987: 103ff.).

It can be argued that since the end of the nineteenth century the basic concepts of liberal and radical democracy have two faces. They are either understood in terms of their classic meaning as founded by Locke and Rousseau, or they are defined in terms of the nineteenth-century materialist theories of utilitarianism and Marxism. Which face actually dominated social and political history made a great difference for the unity and identity which characterizes the variety of historical nation-states. We will specify this view in connection with the social and political history of the Dutch nation-state.

THE DUTCH NATION-STATE AND DEMOCRACY

The struggle for independence against Spanish rule in the sixteenth century was, at the same time, a religious war which laid the foundations of the Netherlands as a Protestant nation. This statement needs some qualification. From its early history the Netherlands was a religiously divided nation. The Protestants were living in the western part of the country, which was the centre of political and economic power, while the Roman Catholics dwelled in the southern provinces. It can be argued that the permanent and often sharp confrontations between Protestants and Roman Catholics in the history of the Netherlands has strengthened the religious consciousness of the Dutch people, which has become a basic characteristic of Dutch national identity.

During the second half of the nineteenth century the political ideas of Locke and Rousseau described above penetrated Dutch society. Firstly, liberal ideas about basic rights, political democracy and state neutrality in religious affairs laid the foundation for the Dutch constitutional state. Within this political framework, labour leaders organized the working class into a political power to achieve an improvement of its standard of life.

Protestant and Roman Catholic leaders in the Netherlands were sceptical about these Enlightenment ideas which were closely associated with the French Revolution and its anti-religious slogan: 'Ni Dieu, ni maître'. This may explain why they accepted ideas of the constitutional state and democracy, but at the same time tried to restrict their influence by founding Christian social and political organizations meant to preserve the traditional norms and institutions in society. It could be argued that until the 1950s, Dutch social and political life was characterized by a balance of influence between Enlightenment political and social ideas on the one hand and traditional norms and institutions which kept the national community together on the other (Daalder 1974: 107ff.).

During the 1960s and 1970s, fundamental social and political changes took place in the Netherlands which laid the foundation of the modern welfare state. During these same decades, first utilitarian liberalism and then Marxism had far-reaching influence on Dutch social and political life.

In line with the expanding economy and wealth, utilitarian liberalism penetrated politics and society during the late 1950s and 1960s. As a result elections tended to become struggles for votes among politicians who one after another promised governmental measures which would guarantee a steady rise in wages for citizens. The high level of prosperity also permitted a generous social security system financed by the government. During these decades the policy of the welfare state brought about a marked decrease in social inequality or a strong increase of social democracy. During the 1970s radical Marxist ideas deeply influenced society and politics. These ideas from the Left raised strong opposition movements against traditional norms and institutions which were considered as ideological barriers against the realization of radical ideals of political participation and emancipation. With ample support of welfare state provisions these movements brought about a strong increase of political equality or political democracy in social and political life.

What role were Christian political parties and social organizations playing during these decades? In fact they spent most of their energy on developing strategies for mutual cooperation to enlarge their position of power and influence in Dutch social and political life. However, at the same time these parties and organizations increasingly neglected the principles from which they originally had arisen. As a result Christian political and social organizations were no real counterforce against prevailing utilitarianism and Marxism but were themselves strongly influenced by these ideologies. So during these decades the balance of influence in Dutch social and political life between Christian norms and institutions on the one hand and social and political Enlightenment ideas on the other was disturbed in favour of the latter, which opened the door to a permanent expansion of the welfare state.

DEMOCRACY AND NATION: CONFLICT OR BALANCE?

It could be argued that it is precisely this permanent or blind extension of the Dutch welfare state that has been the main cause of the growing collective resistance created by this policy, which has even resulted in latent nationalist and anti-democratic sentiments in parts of the population. Elements of that explanation also emerged in the broad public debate which recently started in the media about the moral and social consequences of the welfare state. Leaders of the Liberal and Social Democratic parties, who actively participate in this debate, now openly admit that during the last decades politics have gone too far in realizing the welfare state and the various concepts of democracy it involved. They also acknowledge that in its effects this policy has seriously undermined the integrity and social and moral unity of society. This loss of cohesion in society and the anti-democratic and nationalist reactions it has aroused are now recognized by them as a serious danger for the Dutch constitutional state and democracy.

It strikes me that the political leaders who participate in this debate appeal to the basic ideas of the founding fathers of their political movements as a solution for the problems of social and moral disintegration. Thus leaders of the Social Democratic party recognize that their strong emphasis on welfare state facilities to enlarge chances for emancipation and political participation of citizens may have caused too much envy and competition of interests between individuals and social groups, and hence they propose that government and politics should consciously try to raise feelings of national solidarity and togetherness to regain social and moral cohesion in society. This suggestion is in line with the political ideas of Rousseau described above, which already implied the idea of national sentiments raised by political authorities. On the other hand, the leader of the Liberal party declared that the generosity of the welfare state has in fact resulted in an increase of egoism and individualistic hedonism which, in his opinion, is the main cause of serious problems of social and moral disintegration. He emphasized that society is in need of strong principles of moral integration which, in his opinion, could only be provided by Christian norms and institutions which are part of the nature and history of Dutch society. This position reminds us of course of Locke, who connected his liberal political ideas with the heritage of Christian norms and institutions in his native country.

It can be observed that problems of social and moral disintegration are not limited to Dutch society, but are part of all Western welfare states. These problems have caused a reorientation in modern political theory which has amounted to a reappraising of the concept of the nation as a historically defined social and moral community. So, the neo-liberal political theorist Rawls has redefined the individualistic points of departure which characterized his theory of justice, and has recently elaborated the idea of an 'overlapping consensus' which should hold American liberal society together (Rawls 1993: 133ff.). On the other hand, the neo-radical political theorist David Miller recognized that 'the socialist tradition is overwhelmingly hostile to nationality as a source of identity' and he proposes a 'rescue operation on behalf of nationality' (Miller 1990: 237). Although their concepts of democracy greatly differ, both Locke and Rousseau recognized that democracy for its continued existence needed to be founded in national communities as moral and social entities. Thus they recognized the necessity of a balanced relationship between their abstract principles of democracy and historically defined national communities.

This idea became violated when the concept of democracy was redefined in terms of the materialist ideologies of utilitarianism and Marxism. These ideologies are blind to the history and meaning of moral and social communities. Both ideologies deeply influenced the process of building-up the Dutch welfare state and other Western welfare states as well. Although it is generally admitted that the modern welfare state was very successful in realizing social and political democracy, it should also be recognized that it blindly undermined the specific nature and unity of this society. For that reason the welfare state at the same time became a source of latent collective frustrations in parts of the Dutch population which were a breeding ground for nationalist and anti-democratic sentiments.

Both Rawls and Miller recognize that the contradiction between democracy and nation should not be solved by neglecting the latter in the name of the former. Dutch experiences teach that such policies raise collective frustrations and political conflicts which could endanger democracy. At the same time, Rawls and Miller make an important step forwards to finding a new balance between democracy and nation in our time. Their approach is in line with the basic ideas of the founding fathers of political philosophy of the Enlightenment who already understood the fundamental truth which is implied in the motto: 'Widersprüche gilt es auszuhalten' (Contradictions are things you have to live with).

REFERENCES

Brocker, M. (1991) 'Wahlrecht und Demokratie in die politische Philosophie John Locke', *Zeitschrift für Politik* 38: 47–63.

Daalder, H. (1974) 'The consociational democracy theme', *World Politics* 26: 605–21.

Dubiel, H. (1990) 'Zivilreligion in der Massendemokratie', *Soziale Welt* 41: 125–43.

Farr, J. (1986) ' "So vile and miserable an estate": The problem of slavery in Locke's political thought', *Political Theory* 14: 263–89.

Held, D. (1987) *Models of Democracy*, Cambridge: Polity Press.

Hinsley, F.H. (1989) *Sovereignty*, Cambridge: Cambridge University Press.

Hobsbawm, E.J. (1990) *Nations and Nationalism since 1780*, Cambridge: Cambridge University Press.

Keohane, N.O. (1978) 'The masterpiece of policy in our century: Rousseau on the morality of the Enlightenment', *Political Theory* 6: 457–84.

Locke, John (1690) *Two Treatises of Government*, Cambridge: Cambridge University Press.

Miller, D. (1990) *Market, State and Community*, Oxford: Clarendon Press.
Oerlemans, J.W. (1988) *Rousseau en de privatisering van het bewustzijn*, Groningen: Wolters-Noordhoff.
Rawls, J. (1993) *Political Liberalism*, New York: Columbia University Press.
Resnick, D. (1984) 'Locke and the rejection of the ancient constitution', *Political Theory* 12: 97–114.
Riley, P. (1991) 'Rousseau's general will: Freedom of a particular kind', *Political Studies* 39: 55–74.
Rousseau, J.-J. (1762) *The Social Contract*, Harmondsworth: Penguin.
Sabine, G.H. and Thorson, T.L. (1973) *A History of Political Theory*, Fort Worth: Holt, Rinehart and Winston.
Sap, J.W. (1993) *Wegbereiders der revolutie*, Groningen: Wolters-Noordhoff.
Zvesper, J. (1984) 'The utility of consent in John Locke's political philosophy', *Political Studies* 32: 55–67.

6

PUNISHMENT OR CHILD ABUSE?

Moral Conflicts and Two Levels of Incommensurability

Albert W. Musschenga

It may be true that there are many differences between ethics as a branch of normative, practical philosophy and the social sciences. However, what Anton van Harskamp in his introduction says of the social sciences, i.e. that their aim is not to accumulate knowledge but to contribute to the understanding and solution of human and social conflicts, also applies to ethics, at least as far as general expectations in a pluralistic society are concerned. For the public expects moral philosophers to provide rational, authoritative answers to specific practical problems, especially problems of a collective nature which divide society and threaten its stability.

There are all kinds of moral conflicts. I will concentrate on the most difficult ones: conflicts between adherents to divergent moral traditions. To get clear what moral philosophy could contribute to the solution of such moral conflicts, I will first of all have to analyse more precisely what I understand by a moral conflict.

Three pairs of distinctions are relevant for my understanding of moral conflicts: the distinction between notional and real conflicts, the distinction between virtual and open conflicts, and the distinction between open moral conflicts that involve real (cognitive-)moral disagreements and conflicts that do not.

The distinction between notional and real conflicts comes from Williams. A real conflict (or confrontation: the term that is used by Williams) between two divergent outlooks occurs at a given time if there is a group of people for whom each of the outlooks is a real option. In Williams' view an option is real for a group if it is already their outlook or if they could go over to it; and they could go over to it if they could live inside it in their actual historical circumstances and retain their hold on reality, not engage in extensive self-deception, and so on. A notional conflict occurs when some people know about two divergent outlooks, but at least one of them does not present a real option (Williams 1985: 160). Conflicts between the contemporary Western outlook and those of the past, or of cultures without any contacts, are notional. In an age of media and aircraft nearly all conflicts today are real conflicts.

The second distinction is, within the category of real conflicts, between virtual and open conflicts. A real conflict is an open conflict when at least one of the contestants judges it impossible for divergent beliefs and practices to coexist and then takes action to bring the conflict to a resolution. There are many examples of conflicts which remain virtual. If I despise bribery, I can choose not to do business with people from countries in which it is a normal practice. Real conflicts between persons or groups may also remain virtual if it is for both persons or groups impossible to influence the other's beliefs and practices. The way the Chinese authorities implement their programme of population growth containment is morally disgusting for Western people. Seven-month foetuses are aborted and thrown away in dustbins while they are still alive. There is hardly anything we can do about it. As long as we do not see it with our own eyes, we act as if we do not know.

Whether a virtual conflict evolves into an open one, partly depends on the moral attitude of the contestants. Among the rural Arabs of the West Bank of the Jordan a woman's family and kin are morally dishonoured if she bears a child out of wedlock. The only way to restore honour is to kill her. It does not matter to them whether the pregnancy is due to incest or rape. The man involved does not receive any punishment at all. Only the woman must pay. Her male relatives are morally obligated to kill her. Hatch – from whom I take this example – reports that a small group consisting of Arabs, Christians and Jews has been formed to save these women. The group arranges an abortion for them if they want it, and smuggles them into Europe (Hatch 1983). These people are not forced to interfere; they do it because they see it as a moral obligation.

Sometimes we simply cannot escape dealing with moral conflicts. Large groups of immigrants from countries with non-Western moralities are living in many West European countries. Especially the immigrants from Islamic countries have certain practices that are disapproved of by adherents to the West European morality. Examples are the use of severe corporal punishment in the education of children, the oppression of homosexuals and the unequal treatment of men and women. These immigrant groups are minorities within societies in which the West European morality is dominant. In a country like the Netherlands, discrimination against homosexuals and women is against the law (Article 1 of the Constitution). What used to be differences in moral beliefs and practices between societies with a traditional Islamic morality and societies with a West European morality have become moral conflicts within one society. Notional conflicts have become real conflicts. If real conflicts evolve into open conflicts, one must look for a way to end them. Open conflicts have to be solved.

That question leads us to the third distinction, that between open moral conflicts which involve real (cognitive-)moral disagreements and conflicts that do not. Some, but not all, moral conflicts involve moral disagreements. Conflicts may arise from simple misunderstandings. Suppose I hit someone because I wrongly thought that he was going to attack me. We have a conflict, but not a disagreement. If I accuse someone of having stolen my videorecorder, but he says he borrowed it with my permission, we have a moral conflict, although we do not disagree about the justification of taking away something that belongs to somebody else. Not all disagreements that give rise to a moral conflict are moral disagreements. If a doctor wants to stop a treatment because he deems it futile, and his colleague wants its continuation because he disagrees about the probable effects of the treatment, the disagreement is factual.

It seems plausible to suppose that the typical contribution of moral philosophy to the solution of moral conflicts consists of the analysis of the truth claims of the conflicting moral beliefs. The analysis of the nature of moral justification is the task of that branch of moral philosophy which is called meta-ethics. However, meta-ethics itself turns out to be divided on the question as to whether it is always possible to determine the validity of the truth claims of conflicting moral beliefs, in other words, whether it is possible to find a rational solution for moral disagreements. Absolutist theories contend what relativist theories deny: that it is possible to find rational solutions for moral disagreements. According to relativist theories there exist ultimate, i.e. rationally irresolvable moral disagreements. The moral philosopher who is expected to contribute to the solution of moral conflicts cannot avoid entering the debate between absolutist and relativist theories on the existence of ultimate moral disagreements.

That is why, in the first part of my contribution, I shall throw myself into the debate between absolutism and relativism. I will do so by taking up two questions.

The first question is whether both theories are consistent and plausible. I shall argue that both the conviction that in a moral conflict there ultimately is (or has to be) only one right position (absolutism), and the conviction that a particular moral opinion is always related to a particular culture (relativism), are consistent and plausible. These findings are of consequence for the way absolutism and relativism are 'related' to each other. We may call this relation a relation of incommensurability.

The second question is in what way the two meta-ethical theories have potential for rational, moral conflict resolution? Absolutists and relativists have different perceptions of the nature of moral conflicts. One might think that different perceptions will lead to different therapies. I will show that this is not the case. The rational solution of moral conflicts that is possible according to absolutism can only be found under ideal conditions, which are mostly absent in real life. In most real-life conflicts not all the contestants are ideally rational, well-informed, reasonable, etc. At least some relativists do not deny that in certain cases a rational solution of ultimate moral disagreements can be found. I will show that there is not much difference in the conflict-resolving potential of both theories. In the end, both absolutists and relativists are confronted with the same question: how is one to handle moral conflicts, if there is no solution that is rationally convincing for everyone?

The position one takes in the meta-ethical controversy between absolutism and relativism has consequences for one's view of the tasks of ethics. Absolutists presuppose that the knowledge and the skills of moral philosophers are superior to the common sense moral knowledge of morally well-educated persons, just as scientific knowledge is superior to ordinary, everyday knowledge. I am a relativist who does not believe that ethics can offer rational solutions to moral conflicts. Moral philosophers can only contribute to the quality and the success of discussions about moral conflicts by analysing the nature and the background of conflicts, by making explicit the conflicting values and principles, by scrutinizing the relevance and validity of arguments, and by suggesting rules for handling a conflict. The position which moral philosophers themselves take in a specific conflict is not superior to that of any other moral person; hopefully it will be better argued. As moral persons they argue within the framework of a moral tradition, however fragmented that may be. A moral philosopher like myself, who belongs to a specific moral tradition, and is involved in a moral conflict with an adherent of another tradition, cannot resort to an impartial, tradition-independent, moral point of view. The way he handles a moral conflict under non-ideal conditions depends on the moral beliefs of his own moral tradition. The argument is leading me to the point where it seems necessary to explore the role of the moral beliefs of my own moral tradition.

My moral tradition is that of political liberalism, and so in the second part of this chapter I shall examine the way in which liberalism deals with the kind of moral conflicts which are at stake in a multicultural society. I shall argue that in the last resort liberalism is not, as some of its proponents claim, a purely neutral or purely formal way of conflict resolution; that is to say: it cannot be neutral or formal as far as the allegiance of the moral agent is concerned. We shall see that liberalism is a form of *fideism*.

THE MORAL PHILOSOPHER AS A MORAL AGENT

To illustrate my argument that, in the end, the way even a moral philosopher handles an open moral conflict depends on the moral beliefs of his own tradition, I will build it up around a fictitious but realistic case of a conflict in which I myself am involved. In the last resort I am looking for an answer to the question of what I ought to do in this conflict.

I am acquainted with a fourteen-year-old Moroccan boy who lives in my neighbourhood. I know his family well. The family comes from the region of the Rif mountains – a very traditional part of the country. In that part of Morocco, as in most of the traditional Islamic regions in other countries, corporal punishment is an accepted educational instrument. In Western cultures autonomy and self-realization are the most important educational goals, whereas traditional Islamic education is characterized by discipline. The central concept is '*ql*' which means 'wisdom', in the sense of 'knowing how one ought to behave within the social order'. The children's respect for their parents is more important than their self-respect.

The boy is regularly beaten severely by his father because he does not comply with the mores of his community. In the view of the father, the beating is an unpleasant (for himself, too) but necessary means to discipline his son. In my Western view it is child abuse. The boy wants me to ask his father to stop the beating. I fulfil his request and have a long talk with his father. He is a very severe but just father who is genuinely concerned with the well-being of his children. His conception of the well-being of his children is a traditional Islamic one. I try to convince him with all kinds of arguments: he will destroy the relationship with his son; it is immoral to inflict harm upon children; punishment is not an effective means for reaching his educational goals, and so on. The father is very reasonable; he listens to my arguments, but is not convinced by them. In his view, Moroccan children are used to severe discipline and punishment in their education. For Moroccan fathers, the use of corporal punishment is not only justified, but sometimes it is even morally obligatory if all other means have failed. Not a severe, but a too lenient, education is the reason that children do not learn to respect their culture and even lapse into anti-social and criminal behaviour. So, in the end, the father and I still disagree about the moral quality of the boy's behaviour as well as about the permissibility of severe corporal punishment.

I decide to take the boy to my home and to contact the Board for the Protection of Children. The question that keeps worrying me is whether I am justified in intervening in the father's educational practice. I made it impossible for him to do not just what he *wishes* to do, but what he regards as *justified* and even *obligatory*. Was I right in doing what I did? Are we perhaps both right? If so, I force the father to comply with my morality. For me, as a liberal and as a moral philosopher to whom the peaceful solution of conflicts is the point of ethics, this is hard to accept. Why was it impossible to come to a common understanding with the father? Although I am convinced that I had no other choice, I have a bad conscience. Is it really impossible for both of us to agree on a rational solution?

I have to turn to meta-ethics, hoping that it can help me to explain the nature of the conflict and the causes of my bad conscience, and that it will answer the question of whether it is possible to find a rational solution.

ARE ABSOLUTISM AND RELATIVISM CONSISTENT AND PLAUSIBLE?

A common objection against absolutist theories is that they are implausible because they disregard the cultural diversity of moral beliefs and practices, frequently resulting in moral disagreements. This objection is not valid. A presupposition of this objection is that the empirical observation of moral diversity necessarily leads to meta-ethical relativism. It is certainly evident that meta-ethical relativism is related to cultural relativism. If there were no cultural diversity, there would be no reason to formulate meta-ethical relativist theories. Nevertheless, the fact of moral diversity is a necessary, but not a sufficient, condition for meta-ethical relativism (Barnsley 1972: 340). Absolutists actually do acknowledge cultural and moral diversity. The distinction with relativism has to do with the way of dealing with diversity. In this respect there are two absolutist strategies. The first is that of explaining enduring moral disagreement by postulating deficiencies in the rationality of at least some of the contestants. In the long run, ideally rational people would agree on the right answer to moral questions. The second strategy is to explain disagreements as divergent interpretations and applications of the same basic principles. That is the way many authors have tried to reconcile their belief in a unitary morality with cultural relativism. The usual argument is that the differences in moral beliefs are differences in derivative, not basic, moral beliefs. The differences in derivative beliefs can be explained by referring to differences in non-moral background beliefs. One of the contestants has the wrong beliefs; a fact for which he cannot be blamed. Authors such as Frankena and Rescher hold that there are universally valid – though not universally accepted – principles. Moralities of different times and places may differ in the implementation of these principles (Frankena 1963, 92; Rescher 1989, ch. 1). The conclusion is that absolutism is compatible with the acknowledgement of moral diversity. The consequence of the absolutist position is that it is possible that at least some conventional moralities should be rejected as immoral. That is the reason why absolutism is unattractive for many authors. The 'argument from relativity' is, for example, one of Mackie's arguments against absolutist theories (Mackie 1978: 36). Though absolutism may be unattractive, it is not implausible.

Let us now turn to the question of whether relativism is plausible. We may assume that this question will require more time, simply because relativism is a more complicated theory than absolutism.

Relativists like Harman hold that judgements about actions of persons should be made from the standpoint of the moral conventions of the society of which they are part. Someone who had sex with a woman against her will cannot be condemned as a rapist if he belongs to a society which has not developed the moral notion of rape. Some relativists conclude from the fact of moral diversity that propositions such as 'Blood revenge is wrong' are true and false at the same time. That is an inconsistent and self-contradictory view. Others avoid inconsistency by denying the existence of universal moral truth. In their view it makes no sense to speak of the truth of moral convictions. Moral convictions can be said to be justified, but not to be true. That is the position of Harman. In his view, moral judgements cannot be truth-bearing at all. They do something else: such as express feelings, prescribe a mode of action and so forth (Harman 1989: 363). Margolis, who is also a relativist, refuses to make the concession that moral judgements are not truth-bearing. In his view, a relativist who is himself convinced of the wrongness of blood revenge is not logically obliged to believe that a person with a differing opinion is wrong. 'Why should there be only two truth-values? Suppose there were a third: *Indeterminate*, say, not merely undecided for insufficient evidence? Would there be some mistake or blunder or contradiction or even falsity in so supposing?' (Margolis 1991: 41). 'If the excluded middle,' he says, ' – whether as bivalence or as *tertium non datur* – were "inviolate", then a great many of the well-known charges against relativism would be secured, completely vindicated' (Margolis 1991: 48). Margolis denies that there is a once-and-for-all argument to vindicate the inviolability of the excluded middle. He rejects the kind of relativism that he calls 'relationalism' which relativizes 'truth' and 'falsity' by relationalizing their meaning epistemically *and* by confining the resulting truth-values within suitably compartmentalized spaces of application (ibid.: 10f., 84f., 98f.). He wants to replace the bivalent pair 'true' and 'false' by some set of many-valued truth-values or truth-like values. 'Robust relativism' – his own branch of relativism – does not relativize or relationalize 'truth' and 'falsity'. For robust relativists, moral judgements are truth-bearing. If Margolis is right, relativism is not a logically inconsistent position. It does not necessarily imply that a statement which is false in one tradition can be true in another.

It may be possible to formulate a consistent version of relativism, but is it plausible? Relativists are especially sensitive to the problems of understanding other cultures. They are inclined to say that cultures are incommensurable and that therefore a comparison of cultures is impossible. With Bernstein, I make a distinction between incompatibility, incommensurability and incomparability (Bernstein 1983: 82). Suppose I contend that all human beings are equal, and therefore black and white should have equal opportunities to get jobs and decent houses. My racist neighbour, however, rejects my conclusion because he denies the fundamental equality of human beings. Our convictions are incompatible. They are comparable, though, because they have the same object domain – they deal with the same problem: the allocation of jobs and houses. Although we agree that the principle of equality should be the moral basis for allocating jobs and houses, we fundamentally disagree about the relevance of racial differences. My neighbour has the opinion that black and white should not be treated equally because they differ in morally relevant respects. He believes that God did not create all men as equals. Whites are superior and should govern blacks as God's stewards. So, our convictions are not only incompatible, they are also incommensurable, because there is no common ground between our world views. I reject my neighbour's convictions because I do not understand what he means.

In Bernstein's terminology one has to compare assertions before one can come to the conclusion that they are incompatible and incommensurable. Comparison of one's tradition with another's is only possible, however, if one understands both traditions. Radical semantic relativists claim that the language of some, if not all, moral traditions cannot be translated perfectly into another tradition's language. For them, intranslatability is the mark of incommensurability. It means that the meaning of a term or concept is determined, at least in part, by the network of assumptions with which it is associated. It is impossible to isolate a belief or practice from the network, i.e. the culture, in which it is embedded. Certain terms in at least some other theories or traditions cannot be equated in meaning and reference with any terms in our own theory or tradition. The assertions made in one tradition can be unintelligible in another. We even do not know what a correct translation is. If traditions cannot be translated into each other's, it is impossible to understand another tradition and to compare it with one's own. The most radical conclusion of this argument would be that it is impossible to understand other cultures. Most relativists grant that people can come to understand another culture to a certain extent, at least. A full understanding is perhaps not possible. But what is a full understanding? I doubt whether one can ever fully understand one's own culture, or that of one's partner – or oneself! However, a theory that could not explain the actual possibility of understanding another culture would be implausible.

MacIntyre argues in *Whose Justice? Which Rationality?* that it is possible to learn another language as a 'second first' language (MacIntyre 1988). In order to learn the language of a community, one has to be initiated into its tradition, its beliefs and practices. Learning to understand alien people is learning to understand them in terms of *their* beliefs, values, etc. Only after one has acquired the language of an alien community as one's second first language is it possible to judge whether parts of it are untranslatable into one's first first language. The idea that in principle every assertion and text of another culture can be understood because they can be translated in one's own language might preclude a *real* understanding of those cultures, since in that case there is no room for the recognition of the alien character of some cultures. The recognition that parts of another culture are incommensurable with one's own and cannot be translated into one's own culture does not signify a lack of understanding of that culture. On the contrary, it proves that one has accepted it as a rival to one's own tradition and has not tried to assimilate it.

MacIntyre himself makes a distinction between, on the one hand, languages and traditions which presuppose a well-defined set of beliefs, and on the other hand what he calls 'internationalized languages', of which he says that:

> they are tied very loosely to any particular set of contestable beliefs but are rich in modes of characterization and explanation which enable texts embodying alien schemes of systematic beliefs to be reported on – not in the light of some other rival scheme of belief, by reference of which they would necessarily be exhibited as true or false, reasonable or unreason-

> able, but rather in detachment from all substantive criteria and standards of truth and rationality.
>
> (MacIntyre 1988: 384)

In other words, speakers of 'internationalized languages' think that they can understand 'texts embodying alien schemes of belief' because they think they can translate the texts. But, according to MacIntyre, they do not understand these texts because it is not possible to do justice to alien traditions without recognizing their beliefs as rivals to one's own. Speakers of 'internationalized languages' assimilate while translating. That is, they put the alien tradition's claim to truth for its beliefs between brackets.

Other authors have pointed to the fact that we, as adherents to West European culture, are able to understand and translate the languages of many other cultures because of the richness, ambiguities and multiple sources of our culture (Stout 1988: 65). Wong formulates it as follows: 'When we eventually come to understand the beliefs of another culture that initially look bizarre, we draw from our conception of the range of possible human desire and belief' (Wong 1989: 145).

Our culture is rich and does indeed have many layers and sources. That is why we do not have to assimilate another culture while translating it. In that respect there is a difference between the many-layered Western culture and more homogeneous cultures. Adherents to many of the pre-modern cultures, which still existed a couple of decades ago, could not understand a notion like individual rights. In our culture, we still have a place for notions like honour and merit which figured prominently in earlier periods of our culture. What has changed in the course of the history of our culture, is the strength of such values as honour and merit and their range of application. In the domains of sport and art we still award prizes on the basis of merit, but the level of wages depends on factors like the market value of a job and basic needs for decent living, and to a far lesser extent on the employee's merit. Values like honour and merit have not disappeared, but their validity is much more limited to certain contexts. It is probably easier for us to understand the behaviour of members of pre-modern cultures than it is for members of such cultures to understand our behaviour. They might not be able to translate even the most central concepts of our culture into a language of their own. So at least some relativist theories are able to explain the actual possibility of understanding another culture. In that respect they are not implausible.

I conclude therefore that plausible and consistent versions can be given of both relativism and absolutism. Both types of meta-ethical theories can explain the facts of moral diversity.

It is now plausible to state that absolutism and meta-ethical relativism are themselves incommensurable conceptual frameworks. Preference for one of them probably derives from one's moral or metaphysical beliefs. I cannot elaborate this thesis extensively. I found support for it, however, in MacIntyre and Margolis. MacIntyre rejects the idea of a universal morality. First because it is 'foundationalist', i.e. it wrongly claims to be independent of tradition; there is no reason why the Enlightenment's morality should not be reformulated as a tradition. Second, he rejects that morality because of the intimate connections with liberal individualism, which he abhors (MacIntyre 1981). Margolis's preference for epistemological relativism must be seen in relation to his ontic relativism – his idea that reality is a flux and is constantly changing. His relativism is a prejudice, he says, '. . . a prejudice in the old sense, in the sense of (discerning) the deep performative themes of our operative judgment horizontally formed by the very practice of our historical life' (Margolis 1991: xv).

THE CONFLICT-RESOLVING POTENTIAL OF THE TWO THEORIES

What light does my meta-ethical exploration shed on my conflict with the Moroccan father? Absolutism's explanation is either that the father or myself or both of us are not ideally rational, or that both standpoints are interpretations of the same universally valid principles in diverse social contexts against diverse non-moral background beliefs. In the latter case there might be no ultimate moral disagreement at all between the father and me. If both of us accept an explanation of that kind, this might result in a willingness to scrutinize not only the other's, but also one's own, reasons and beliefs. There is a chance that we might end the conflict by solving the underlying disagreement. Unless both of us are willing to accept that explanation, the real moral conflict will continue, as our convictions are practically incompatible.

Relativism's explanation is that we may not agree because we do not understand each other. We will both have to learn the language of the other's tradition before being able to conclude that our convictions are comparable and incommensurable. Relativists do not necessarily deny that a rational solution for real moral disagreements is possible. MacIntyre is an example. He argues that the adherents to one tradition can learn the language of another tradition as a second first language. In his view it is also possible for the adherents to one tradition to come to recognize another as superior. How is that compatible with his central thesis that a rational moral enquiry is only possible within the conceptual framework of a tradition? With Kuhn, MacIntyre believes that conflicts between scientific theories cannot be resolved through research guided by a neutral, theory-independent methodology. There is no such methodology. In an analogous way, conflicts between moral traditions cannot be solved by an appeal to tradition-independent universal standards.

There is, however, an important difference between the views of Kuhn and MacIntyre. MacIntyre criticized Kuhn's idea of the transition from one paradigm to another. Kuhn characterized such a transition as a 'conversion experience'. MacIntyre and others concluded from this that he regarded scientific revolutions as non-rational or irrational, a conclusion Kuhn himself has never drawn. In scientific revolutions, according to MacIntyre, adherents to a paradigm meet a problem they cannot answer adequately according to the criteria of their own epistemological ideals (MacIntyre 1989: 256). In such a situation, a paradigm lapses into incoherence. An epistemological crisis emerges. A new paradigm is needed, not only to solve the problem in question, but also to explain why the old one turned out to be inadequate. So, according to MacIntyre, the transition from one paradigm to another – better described as the development of a new paradigm by adherents to an old one – is quite a rational process. Epistemological crises also occur within moral traditions. Every tradition has its agenda of unresolved problems. It may happen that a tradition, judged by its own criteria, ceases to make progress in resolving these problems. For example, it may no longer be able to settle conflicts about rival solutions for a problem. The tradition then falls into an epistemological crisis. A solution is possible only by what MacIntyre calls 'imaginative conceptual innovation': the development of enriched theoretical and conceptual structures. One source of innovation is the forgotten layers of the tradition itself. A crisis can also make the adherents to a tradition open and sensitive to the claims of a rival tradition. If they have succeeded in understanding the beliefs and the way of life of this rival tradition, they may come to recognize that its concepts and theories offer a solution for the problem and an explanation for the failure of their own tradition (MacIntyre 1988: 361–6). So the confrontation with rival traditions is the second source for the innovation of conceptual structures. The solutions that are found in a process of conceptual innovation are rational, not from a point of view that is independent from tradition, but from the tradition of those who were involved in the conflict.

MacIntyre's analysis of the solution of moral conflicts is not applicable to what he himself calls 'fundamental disagreements', which are disagreements *between* moral traditions. In his view, a moral tradition will only open itself towards other traditions when its own resources turn out to be inadequate to solve internal problems. In such a situation it becomes incoherent. However, it never lapses into incoherence simply because of the existence of rival answers within other traditions. My views on education and the use of physical punishment are rivals to those that are held by the Moroccan father. The confrontation as such between him and me does not need to cause a crisis in his moral views.

Whether or not a moral conflict has a cognitive core, whether or not one believes that it is – at least in principle, under ideal conditions – possible to find a rational solution, real moral conflicts like the one between the Moroccan father and myself have to be brought to an end. There are three ways out: one is violent and two are peaceful. If the conflict is solved the violent way, the more powerful contestant forces the other to comply with his morality. In the second, peaceful, way one of the parties is converted to the position of the other. The other peaceful solution is that the parties are able to find a way in between their conflicting positions. The preference for one of these strategies has hardly anything to do with one's meta-ethical convictions. Though meta-ethics may be relevant for understanding moral conflicts and for one's attitude towards such conflicts, it has little significance for their practical solution.

Some relativist social anthropologists are of the opinion that relativism favours a tolerant attitude towards other cultures. Philosophers such as Harrison have shown, however, that relativism does not necessarily imply tolerance (Harrison 1982). Tolerance is a substantial moral principle. Meta-ethical absolutists as well as meta-ethical relativists can be tolerant towards people with different practices, if that principle is part of their morality. Both will be intolerant if that is not the case. Even tolerant moralities will forbid some practices such as slavery, blood revenge or the burning of widows. If someone had to decide about interfering in such a practice in order to save a life, it would, in my view, not make any difference whether he were a meta-ethical absolutist or a meta-ethical relativist. Meta-ethical absolutists as well as meta-ethical relativists will agree that such decisions have to be defined from the point of view of that person's own morality.

The way someone handles moral conflicts in practice will be influenced by the moral beliefs of his tradition. So I will have to leave the debate between absolutism and relativism behind and consult my own moral tradition, that of political liberalism.

LIBERAL CONFLICT RESOLUTION

The dominant political morality in West European countries is that of political liberalism. Liberal political morality says that people should be free to live according to their own ideas and values, as long as they do not harm others, i.e. cause a setback to their interests which is wrong (Feinberg 1984: 36), even if those ideas and values are regarded as immoral and demeaning. According to the liberal core principle of tolerance, moral disapproval of a practice is not a sufficient argument for interference. 'Toleration is the virtue of refraining from exercising one's power to interfere with others' opinion and action although that deviates from one's own over something important and although one morally disapproves of it' (Nicholson 1985: 162). All actions that are not harmful to others are regarded as private and fall outside the scope of legitimate state intervention.

Central to liberal political morality is the division of society into a public and a private sphere. Metaphorically speaking, liberalism places a wall within society between two zones (Walzer 1984). This wall is not a spatial but a normative separation. For many people, sexual behaviour is private, not only in the normative, but also in the spatial sense. They have the right to decide when, how and with whom to make love, and moreover they usually prefer not to be seen by others when doing it. Most actions are only private in the normative sense. We ourselves choose how to dress – that is a private matter – but we like to show our clothes in public. Citizens are free to discuss private matters in public. The contrast with public matters, however, is that there is no need to come to a consensus. Liberals make a distinction between matters in which (positive) consensus about the right approach is necessary, and matters in which one can agree to disagree (which I will call a negative consensus). By making this distinction, political liberalism does not solve moral conflicts. It simply removes them from the political agenda. Liberals do not have to agree about, for example: the value of pornography, the meaning of life, or the value and the truth of belief in God. The list of questions about which a liberal society has to reach a positive consensus is shorter than in non-liberal societies. The length of that list is context-dependent. Some liberal societies might consider the preservation of their cultural inheritance a collective good which can only be entrusted to the State, while others leave initiatives in that domain to social groups and to the market. Issues which will appear in every list are those which Rawls calls 'primary social goods', goods which are necessary for everybody, regardless of their life-plan: rights and liberties, opportunities and powers, income and wealth, and the social basis for self-respect (Rawls 1972: 90 ff.).

Education is one of the fields which in the liberal view belongs to the private sphere. Parents have the right to determine how they educate their children and which educational goals they strive for. As is the case with other zones of action, the freedom of parents in educating their children is limited by the harm principle. Parents are not free to inflict harm upon their children.

It seems to be clear what I, as a liberal, have to do in my conflict with the Moroccan father. His use of corporal punishment evidently does cause harm to his son. I have no choice but to report this case to the authorities. However, anyone who reads the anthropological literature about educational practices in diverse cultures will see how divergent the beliefs about goals and means of education are. Practices which are regarded as beneficial in our culture are seen as harmful in other cultures. The definition of child abuse is not merely an empirical matter; it is infused by cultural beliefs about what constitutes well-being for children (Korbin 1980).

The use of corporal punishment is broadly accepted in some cultures, such as that of the father in my imaginary case. Those who reject corporal punishment as an acceptable means in education will perhaps not characterize every instance in which it is used as child abuse. Everybody will have his own 'grey zone'. However, it goes without saying that someone who regards corporal punishment as normal will draw the limit between punishment and child abuse at a different place from someone who rejects corporal punishment categorically. There will evidently be cases which are regarded by people from a 'modern' Western culture as child abuse, while, for example, a traditional Moroccan father will speak of an inevitable severe punishment which has to prevent his child from moral depravation.

Educational methods are an essential part of the educational culture of a group. Physical punishments fit into an education that aims at the integration of a child into his own cultural group and his subordination to that group. The question now becomes whether political liberalism can take the fact of the cultural definition of child abuse into account. Or is it so intimately connected with Western culture that it cannot leave room for cultures which disagree with its views on education?

Some liberals – whom I will call 'traditional liberals' – believe in the absolute primacy of individual rights. Others – whom I call 'moderate' liberals – believe that traditional liberalism's emphasis on individual rights is too strong. Their argument is that people not only grow and mature within communities, which they leave as soon as they become adults. They believe that individuals need embedding in forms of communal living in order to flourish and to become happy. Membership of communities is, in their view, even partly constitutive of the identity of individuals.

These moderate liberals plead for the assignment of group rights to local communities which enable them to preserve those moral practices which they regard as essential for their communal living, and to avert practices which they regard as a threat to the survival of their culture. Group rights form a buffer against the interference of the State with a community's way of life. They can also confer power on a community to prohibit certain practices by members which are considered to be detrimental to its way of life. One could imagine that these rights would confer the power on the local authorities of a small town – such as the Dutch town of Staphorst, a place with a conservative Christian majority and a distinctive culture – to prohibit the disturbance of Sunday as a day of rest, swearing, and the selling and buying of pornography.

Individual rights protect the goods and interests of individuals. It is common usage to make a distinction between individual goods and interests, on the one hand, and public goods and interests, on the other. Schools, infrastructural provisions such as a sewage systems, roads, etc., and also some form of social security, are goods that, while public in nature, eventually serve the interests of individuals, whatever their plan of life or conception of the good. These public goods have to be distinguished from what authors like Postema call 'collective goods'. Collective goods constitute 'the moral climate', the common good, the collective identity of a community. That common good is not purely instrumental to the interests of a community's members. It precedes the private good of these members and even partly defines it. Membership of a community and taking part in its collective goods is an important aspect of the personal identity of the individual members. Examples of such a collective good are the language of a community, the land where it lives, or the common religion with its beliefs and practices (Postema 1987). It is the function of group rights to protect the collective goods of a community, i.e. its cultural and moral identity.

It is argued that the assignment of group rights to communities is *ipso facto* not liberal, because these rights limit the freedom of individuals, whether they are dissenting members of the community or outsiders who visit the community, to behave in accordance with their conception of the good. The reply of the moderate, non-individualistic liberal would be that no one is forced to live in or to visit a town like Staphorst. Dissenters are not compelled by prohibitions like those mentioned above, to lead a way of life that is in conflict with their fundamental convictions. Nor are their fundamental interests affected. Only their freedom of choice in rather unimportant matters is limited.

According to the moderate liberals, in a conflict between group rights and individual rights, individual rights do not necessarily always prevail. By virtue of what can a morality which recognizes group rights claim to be liberal? Some of the individual rights are so constitutive of the identity of a liberal political community, such as freedom of conscience, freedom of religion, freedom of the Press, and freedom from discrimination, that they cannot give way to group rights. These rights are to be regarded as collective goods which are constitutive of a liberal political community. The common good of the political community has priority over that of local communities. The implication could be that a liberal government grants local communities the right to, say, prohibit activities which they regard as a disturbance of Sunday as a day of rest, but not the right to prohibit homosexual practices, because non-discrimination is held to be an essential element of the political community's moral climate.

Is it possible that immigrant groups in the Netherlands, like the Moroccans, claim a group right for the protection of their educational culture? Should intervention in educational practices be seen as an infringement of an institution that is essential for the preservation and transmission of traditional Moroccan culture? As I said before, educational culture is an essential part of a community's culture. It could be argued that it should be left to a community itself to determine whether practices like the use of corporal punishment are central to its educational culture.

In my view, a freedom to inflict severe physical punishment cannot be compared with a right to prohibit pornography or activities that disturb the rest on Sunday. Children are in various respects – financial, emotional – dependent on their parents. They do not have the opportunity to choose parents with other educational practices. The right of children to physical integrity should weigh more heavily for liberals than the interests of a community in the preservation of its culture. One could even argue that the protection of children is a collective good of a liberal political community. My provisional conclusion is therefore that a moderate, non-individualistic liberalism can give local communities room for the preservation of their cultural identity. There are, however, limits. In the end, in a country such as the Netherlands, these limits are drawn in terms of the Western culture with which political liberalism is connected. Even if I am a moderate, non-individualistic liberal, it will be my duty to report a case of severe physical punishment, which is regarded as child abuse in my culture, to the authorities.

PUBLIC JUSTIFICATION AND RESPECT FOR PERSONS

Why is it that I am not happy with this conclusion? I do not agree with those who argue that one has to start from the definition which a culture itself gives of child abuse, because every culture aims at the well-being of its children. They only want the State in a multicultural society to intervene in those cases which are regarded as child abuse according to the group to which the parents belong. However, I take it to heart when someone states that I am an ethnocentrist who has no proof for his belief in the superiority of his culture.

My hunch is that my bad conscience has something to do with my liberal ideas about neutrality and public justification. Larmore refers the liberal demand for public justification to the obligation of equal respect for persons. We should never treat other persons as mere objects of our will, even when we reject their beliefs. We are under the obligation to explain to them our actions which also affect them. 'To show another equal respect is to treat his demand for justification as part of a rational discussion one must have with him' (1987: 65). We cannot stop the conversation the moment we run into a difference of opinion. In such a situation we have to withdraw to neutral ground in order to try to solve the conflict. That is what Larmore calls a 'common norm of rational argument'. However, I did try to find a common ground between myself and the Moroccan father, and did not succeed.

Liberals make a distinction between respect for persons and respect for beliefs. One can have respect for the integrity of someone of whose convictions one disapproves. This distinction is also made by Larmore. I can have respect for the earnestness and sincerity with which my Moroccan father tries to educate his children, without respecting the convictions that guide him in his educational activities. However, I can only draw a boundary between respect for persons and respect for beliefs if I find the beliefs that I reject irrational. An absolutist would regard the father's belief as primitive and irrational. As a relativist, who is convinced that rationality depends on context, I disapprove of the father's action and reject his beliefs, but I have no ground to qualify his beliefs as irrational.

What if the father were Dutch, and not Moroccan? Would that make a difference? If I informed against a Dutch father, I would not have a bad conscience. Why not? In both cases I am co-responsible for limiting their freedom of action. The difference is that if the father were Dutch, I could justify my decision to him because I have good reason to suppose that we share the same public culture. By justifying my decision to him in terms of a shared public culture, I do justice to the principle of respect for persons, even if I contribute to the restriction of his freedom. But I cannot justify my decision to the Moroccan father in terms that are acceptable for him. As a relativist, I cannot prove that my morality is superior to his. From his point of view, he is simply forced to comply with liberal morality without any good reason. If I were an absolutist, I would feel sorry for the father, but without having a bad conscience. After all, I did not infringe on the principle of respect for persons. Probably I had the conviction that in the end, after having learned the right beliefs, the father would retrospectively agree with my decision. As a relativist I cannot but have a bad conscience because I made it impossible for the rational, reasonable and good-willing father to act in accordance with his deepest convictions. My relativist liberalism is the explanation for my bad conscience.

The difference between an absolutist and a relativist liberal is not that only the former will force others to comply with his moral convictions. Both will do this if it is impossible to let divergent moral practices coexist side by side. Liberals are not tolerant because they are relativists. Relativism supports tolerance in combination with the liberal idea of legitimacy. Only the relativist liberal will have a bad conscience when he forces others to comply with his own morality. A political liberalism that is infused by relativism leads to a deeper respect for people with divergent, non-liberal beliefs and practices. The difference between an absolutist and a relativist liberal is that the absolutist has to deny his opponents' claim to truth for their moral convictions. If I am right that it is impossible to make a strict separation between respect for persons and respect for beliefs, relativist liberalism does foster respect for persons with divergent moral convictions.

Is there any difference between the attitude of a pre-modern society towards outsiders and the attitude of a modern, liberal community? Many pre-modern societies admitted outsiders as 'brothers' if they were willing to conform to the society's customs and practices. The main difference is that a liberal community is morally obliged to offer everybody the protection of its morality, and to let everybody share in its benefits and advantages. One does not have to be accepted as a member of the historical community of a liberal society – as a 'brother' – to enjoy the protection of the liberal morality. Still, an object of protection is not an equal participant in the public moral debate. Children are no more than objects of protection until they are old enough and fully socialized into our moral resources to participate in the public debate. Does a liberal society treat 'strangers' as children until they are able to speak the language of the liberal moral tradition? In a way it does.

As a relativist liberal I agree with Postema that justification is context-dependent. As Postema formulates it: 'Justification must be rooted in a company of persons marked by some degree of common practice and experience. It must form the point of departure and point of reference for public argument. The aim is to articulate which is, between them, already public' (Postema 1991: 174). In an earlier article Postema writes that public justification must draw on the normative resources that are available to a historical community. A public debate is a historical enterprise; participants see themselves as 'joining an argument already underway' (Postema 1989: 122). Although as a liberal I am morally obliged to treat the Moroccan father as a full and equal member of the moral community, he is not a member of my historical community. He and I do not have a common history and the same moral resources. If justification is indeed context-dependent, I and the other members of my historical community cannot but justify our actions by interpreting our common moral resources. That also applies to our actions regarding persons who are not members of our historical community. If my act of disrespect for the father's authority over his son can be justified in terms of the moral resources of my historical community, it was the right thing to do, whether or not the justification is accepted by the father. So although we regard the father as an equal member of the moral community, we do not treat him as a full member: he is not a subject in, but an object of our public moral debate. He can only become a participant in that debate if he is willing to speak the language of our moral tradition as his second first language.

WHY POLITICAL LIBERALISM CANNOT REFRAIN FROM CLAIMING TRUTH FOR ITS CONVICTIONS

Rorty characterizes his relation to political liberalism as 'liberal irony'. An 'ironist' is someone who has radical and continuing doubts about the 'final vocabulary' he currently uses: (1) because he has been impressed by other vocabularies taken as final by people he has encountered; (2) he realizes that arguments phrased in his present vocabulary can neither underwrite nor dissolve these doubts; and (3) in so far as he philosophizes about his situation, he does not think his vocabulary is closer to reality than others, that it is in touch with a power not himself (Rorty 1989: 73). A liberal ironist combines his commitment with a sense of the contingency of his commitment (idem: 61). Liberal political freedoms cannot and need not be based '. . . on a view about universally shared human ends, human rights, the nature of rationality, the Good for Man, nor anything else'. 'We ironists who are also liberals think that such freedoms require no consensus on any topic more basic than their own desirability.' The social glue which holds the liberal society together '. . . consists in little more than a consensus that the point of social organization is to let everybody have a chance at self-creation to the best of his or her abilities, and that that goal requires, besides peace and wealth, the "standard bourgeois freedoms" ' (idem: 84).

For practical reasons it is important that liberalism does not claim to be a metaphysical doctrine. The argument is that a political morality which is based on controversial metaphysical doctrine could never resolve conflicts between religions and other metaphysical worldviews. A debate on the ultimate, true grounds of liberalism obviates its political function.

In Rawls's view, comprehensive conceptions of the good are incommensurable. This means 'we are to recognize the practical impossibility of reaching reasonable and workable political agreement in judgment on the truth of comprehensive doctrines, especially an agreement that might serve the political purpose, say, of achieving peace and concord in a society characterized by religious and philosophical differences' (Rawls 1993: 63). Justice as fairness, his political conception of justice, should only serve as a basis for an agreement between informed and willing political persons viewed as free and equal persons. Political liberalism does not refer to its conception of justice as true, it refers to it only as reasonable.

I agree with Raz that it is impossible to recommend a conception of justice without claiming truth for it. Even if one assumes that the goal of political philosophy is purely practical and that it is not concerned with establishing evaluative truths, one accepts some truths such as the presuppositions which make the enterprise intelligible, for example, the truth of the values such as social unity and stability based on a consensus (and not on force and violence) (Raz 1990: 14). 'To recommend one [theory] as a theory of justice for our societies is to recommend it as a just theory of justice, that is, as a true, or reasonable, or valid theory of justice' (ibid.: 15).

As I argued on pp. 105–6, a relativist ethical theory does not necessarily refrain from the claim that moral statements are truth-bearing. Political liberalism even has to claim truth for its convictions, if it is to remain true to its intentions. I will explain why this is the case. The liberal morality of human rights is universal in intent: it has an in-built drive to transcend the boundaries of historical liberal communities. The ideal historical liberal community encompasses all members of the moral community of human persons. A liberal cannot be satisfied until the moral community and the historical liberal community coincide. Rorty's liberalism is not a group morality: it is cosmopolitan. 'The right way to take the slogan "we have obligations to human beings simply as such" is as a means of reminding ourselves to keep trying to widen our sense of "us" as far as we can' (Rorty 1989: 196). It is a very limited form of cosmopolitanism, however, compared to the ideals of the human rights movement. Rorty speaks about the liberals' obligations towards strangers, not about the rights of strangers. The human rights movement sees the liberal freedoms as human rights. The duty to respect these rights binds all human beings, not only the members of the historical community of liberals. A human rights' activist is a missionary. An ironist is the antipode of a missionary. Why should human rights' activists, whom I regard as the liberals par excellence, commit themselves to propagate the idea of universal human rights if they were not convinced of its validity and truth?

Liberal political morality is historical in a double sense. First, it aims at the universal acceptance of its convictions. Second, it is the fruit of historical experiences, the outcome of the collective experiments in peaceful coexistence of adherents to diverse, conflicting religious and moral traditions. I will come back to that in the last section. Liberal morality cannot be convincingly justified to those who do not share these experiences. Those who live in pervasively pluralistic societies will sooner or later discover that there is no peaceful alternative to liberal morality. In Rorty's words, they will sooner or later agree on the social desirability of liberal freedoms. A Rortyan liberal will wait until history teaches countries like Iran its lessons. A human rights' activist cannot wait. If he did, he would experience that as a betrayal of his belief in the universal validity of the liberal ideas about human dignity. In confrontations with people outside the liberal tradition who do not share the same public culture, there is no other alternative but to expound a view on the nature of a human being and the society that supports the liberal principles. Why should a liberal not appeal to common features of human nature, as long as he concedes that they are constructed within culture-dependent and therefore 'contingent' webs of concepts and beliefs (Reeder 1993: 197)?

Authors like Rorty and Rawls are right when arguing that it is neither possible nor necessary to found liberal political morality on a metaphysical doctrine that is acceptable to all of liberalism's adherents. Political liberalism can be supported by various grounds derived from the diverse comprehensive doctrines in which it is embedded. Rawls himself also admits that in affirming a political conception of justice we may eventually have to assert at least certain aspects of our own comprehensive or philosophical doctrine. This is unavoidable, for example, when someone insists that certain questions are so fundamental for him that to ensure their being rightly settled justifies civil strife (Rawls 1993: 152). In a confrontation with adherents to theocratic religious moral traditions which deny the idea of human rights, we cannot but resort to our comprehensive conceptions of the person and of society in order to justify the truth of our political convictions.

BEYOND RELATIVISM?

The overlapping consensus about the political principles of liberalism that exists in pluralist democratic societies is not the result of rational acceptance of the truth of the liberal convictions. Liberal morality is the more or less contingent outcome of a historical struggle to find a common basis for coexistence between groups with different religious traditions. All parties were well aware that they had to find such a common basis in order to arrive at peaceful coexistence. After all, they were condemned to each other in a way. None of the traditions had a ready-made solution for the problem of the coexistence of groups with conflicting conceptions of the good. However, there is no better proof of the possibility of dialogue and peaceful coexistence than practice itself. Roman Catholics experienced that it was possible for Protestants to be loyal citizens. The real-life experiences of dialogue and coexistence called for reflection and interpretation. These experiences were interpreted in terms of values such as equality of freedom, freedom of conscience, autonomy, mutual respect and tolerance. These values did not come out of the blue, of course: they were already present in the works of philosophers like Erasmus and John Locke. Subsequently, these values were integrated into the various moral traditions. Thus, liberal morality is an overlapping consensus between diverse moral traditions; it is the result of a historical process in which none of the rival traditions remained unchanged.

It is inevitable that groups with non-liberal moral traditions, who did not participate in the process of consensus building, will not always experience the liberal morality of a society as neutral. For these groups there is no other way than to start a dialogue with the dominant groups when they think that their way of life is unequally affected by certain laws and practices. As a result of such a dialogue, a liberal society may, for instance, exempt an Islamic minority group from complying with a certain statutory regulation, so that they can conform to the rules of the Hadith concerning ritual slaughter, even if the method prescribed by the Hadith causes the animal more pain than the legally sanctioned one. This has happened in the Netherlands. The immigration of new groups can have the consequence that existing laws and policies can no longer be considered as neutral. A new public debate has to throw light on the question of whether the goods favoured by these laws and policies are an essential element of that society's liberal morality. The host society must be willing to start a discussion on elements of the overlapping consensus. The appearance of Islamic ethno-cultural groups in countries like the Netherlands necessitates the reinterpretation of the liberal tradition of morality. This shows that the overlapping consensus is not static, but dynamic. The newcomers have no choice but to participate in that discussion on the basis of the two presuppositions of the liberal solution for plurality: the separation between a public and a private sphere, and between a common political morality and diverse conceptions of the good.

I am bound to do what I am obliged to do according to my own liberal morality: to protect the son against his father. At the same time, respect for persons and other principles of liberal morality tell me that I must be willing to begin a dialogue with the father and the other adherents to his morality about all the practices and institutions of our liberal morality and liberal democracy which they regard as unnecessarily oppressive. It is impossible to predict what the outcome of such a dialogue on specific points will be. One of the reasons is that in a real dialogue participants often change not only their opinions, but also change in a more radical way.

Bernstein regards dialogue and conversation as a third way beyond relativism and absolutism or objectivism. He sees relativism as the dialectical antithesis to absolutism that ran too far (Bernstein 1983: 166f.). I disagree with him on this point. Dialogue in the field of ethics is not a way beyond relativism and absolutism. It is not a meta-ethical, but a normative, ethical concept. Dialogue is an approach to moral conflicts which is characteristic of the liberal moral tradition.

I argued that relativism does not necessarily lead to dialogue and tolerance. It can, however, strengthen and foster an already accepted principle of tolerance. My branch of relativism is one in which it is not necessary to refrain from claiming truth for one's moral conviction. I showed why it is even impossible for political liberals who believe in the equal dignity of all human beings not to claim truth for that conviction. However, the acceptance of that truth is not rationally required. This insight has implications for the way I would describe my allegiance to political liberalism. In the relativist interpretation, a liberal's commitment to his political morality is a form of *fideism* – a term also used by Rorty (Rorty 1991: 185). This view places moral belief on the same level as religious belief. As a person with a Calvinist upbringing, I am taught not to worry if someone succeeds in undermining my reasons for believing in God. That standpoint is nicely formulated by Plantinga: 'From Calvin's point of view believing in the existence of God on the basis of rational argument is like believing in the existence of your spouse on the basis of the analogical argument for other minds – whimsical at best and unlikely to delight the person concerned' (Plantinga 1983: 67f.). The ground of Christian belief is man's personal encounter with the self-revealing God. Analogously, the final grounds for the belief in liberalism are not constituted by rational arguments about human nature, but are derived from historical experiences. Rational arguments can support beliefs, but they are not decisive for their acceptance.

REFERENCES

Barnsley, J. (1972) *The Social Reality of Ethics*, London: Routledge & Kegan Paul.

Bernstein, R. J. (1983) *Beyond Objectivism and Relativism*, Oxford: Blackwell.

Feinberg, J. (1984) *Harm to Others: The Moral Limits to Criminal Law*, Vol. I, New York: Oxford University Press.

Frankena, W. K. (1963) *Ethics*, Englewood Cliffs: Prentice Hall.

Harman, G. (1989) 'Is there a single true morality?', in M. Krausz (ed.) *Relativism: Interpretation and Confrontation*, Notre Dame/London: University of Notre Dame Press, 363–86. Reprinted from D. Copp and D. Zimmermann (eds) (1984), *Morality, Reason and Truth: New Essays on the Foundations of Ethics*, Totowa, NJ: Rowman & Allenheld, 27–48.

Harrison, G. (1982) 'Relativism and tolerance', in M. Krausz and J.W. Meiland (eds) *Relativism: Cognitive and Moral*, Notre Dame/London: University of Notre Dame Press, 229–44. Reprinted from (1976) *Ethics* 86: 122–35.

Hatch, E. (1983) *Culture and Morality,* New York: Columbia University Press.

Korbin, J. E. (1980) 'The cultural context of child abuse and neglect', *Child Abuse and Neglect* 4: 1–13.

Larmore, C. (1987) *Patterns of Moral Complexity,* Cambridge: Cambridge University Press.

MacIntyre, A. (1981) *After Virtue,* Notre Dame: University of Notre Dame Press.

—— (1988) *Whose Justice? Whose Rationality?* London: Duckworth.

—— (1989) 'Epistemological crisis, dramatic narratives and the philosophy of science', in S. G. Clarke (ed.) *Anti-Theory in Ethics and Moral Conservatism*, Albany: State University of New York Press, 241–63. Reprinted from (1977) *The Monist* 60: 453–72.

Mackie, J. L. (1978) *Inventing Right and Wrong,* Harmondsworth: Penguin.

Margolis, J. (1991) *The Truth about Relativism*, Cambridge, MA: Blackwell.

Nicholson, P. (1985) 'Toleration as a moral ideal', in J. Horton and S. Mendus (eds) *Aspects of Toleration*, London/New York: Methuen, 158–73.

Plantinga, A. (1983) *Reason and Belief,* Notre Dame: University of Notre Dame Press.

Postema, G. (1987) 'Collective evils, harms, and the law', *Ethics* 97: 414–40.

—— (1989) 'In defense of "French nonsense" – fundamental rights in jurisprudence', in N. MacCormick and Z. Bankowski (eds) *Enlightenment, Rights and Revolutions*, Aberdeen: Aberdeen University Press, 107–33.

—— (1991) 'Public faces – private places. Liberalism and the enforcement of morals', in A.W. Musschenga, B. Voorzanger and A. Soeteman (eds) (1991), *Morality, Worldview, and Law*, Assen: Van Gorcum, 153–77.

Rawls, J. (1972) *A Theory of Justice*, London: Oxford University Press.

—— (1993) *Political Liberalism*, New York: Columbia University Press.

Raz, J. (1990) 'Facing adversity: the case of epistemic abstinence', *Philosophy and Public Affairs* 19: 3–47.

Reeder, J. P. Jr. (1993) 'Foundations without foundationalism', in G. Outka and J. P. Reeder Jr. (eds) *Prospects for a Common Morality*, Princeton: Princeton University Press, 191–215.

Rescher, N. (1989) *Moral Absolutes*, New York: Lang.

Rorty, R. (1989) *Contingency, Irony, and Solidarity*, Cambridge: Cambridge University Press.

—— (1991) 'The priority of democracy to philosophy', in *Objectivity, Relativism, and Truth*, Philosophical Papers, Vol. I, Cambridge: Cambridge University Press, 197–202. Reprinted from M. Peterson and R. Vaughan (eds) (1988), *The Virginia Statute of Religious Freedom*, Cambridge: Cambridge University Press, 257–88.

Stout, J. (1988) *Ethics after Babel: The Languages of Morals and Their Discontents*, Boston: James Clark & Company.

Walzer, M. (1984) 'Liberalism and the art of separation', *Political Theory* 12: 315–31.

Williams, B. (1985) *Ethics and the Limits of Philosophy*, London: Fontana Press/Collins.

Wong, D. B. (1989) 'Three kinds of incommensurability', in M. Krausz (ed.) *Relativism: Interpretation and Confrontation,* Notre Dame: University of Notre Dame Press, 140–58.

7

ON THE OBJECTIVITY OF JUDICIAL DECISIONS

P. W. Brouwer

In 1985 a number of articles in the gospel magazine *Evan*, published by the L. and J. Goeree Evangelical Foundation and distributed from door to door, led to numerous judicial pronouncements. The import of the articles was remarkable. The message of the two evangelists was that members of the Jewish people, at least those observing the Jewish faith, were themselves responsible for the suffering wrought upon them through the ages, in particular the atrocities committed during the Nazi regime. This religious conviction was based on an interpretation of words spoken in Matthew 27:25 during the trial of Jesus: 'His blood be on us, and on our children.' In the words of the Goerees, 'With the blood Jesus shed to deliver them, the Jews brought their own destruction upon themselves. They murdered their redeemer. They rejected the salvation God was offering them. They rejected life and opted for death. No nation would have been able to do Israel any harm if it had recognized its prince of peace. Had they accepted their Messiah, the Jews would not have become a victim of the nations.'

That the Jews were thus blamed, however, did not mean that the injustice done to them was justified and that those who wrought it were absolved. The Goerees themselves also said that this was a case of horrific injustice. They spoke, for example, of 'bestial murder'. No denial can be read in such wording of the murderers' guilt. The Goerees' opinions do, therefore, leave room for a kind of 'religious' guilt beside the more worldly guilt of the perpetrators. In addition, their standpoint was, to their minds, prompted by concern for the fate of Jews. These would, after conversion, be indemnified against persecution, which in their opinion was proved by the 'fact' that, during the last World War, 'only those Jews were spared that were converted to Jesus'.

In this article, I will discuss the criminal prosecution of L. Goeree and the arguments that can be put forward in a judicial context for or against that legal action, trial and conviction. The charge made was that of an infringement of Section 137e, subsection 1, number 1 of the Dutch Penal Code, which read at the time:

> Anyone who, other than for the purpose of factual reporting, promulgates a statement that he knows or within reason should suspect to be an insult to a group of people because of their race, religion or philosophy of life or an incitement to hate or discriminate against people or to commit violent acts against people or goods of people because of their race, religion or philosophy of life, will be punished with a prison sentence of at most six months or a third-category fine.[1]

At first sight there was little unanimity among the courts. The District Court Zwolle arrived at a verdict of 'guilty' because of the seriously offensive nature of the statements.[2] In view of the absence of malicious intent on the part of the defendant, however, no punishment was meted out, nor measures taken. The Court of Appeal Arnhem, in the second instance, was of the opinion that the statements made did not constitute an insult, as they were not gratuitously offensive or hurtful.[3] On the one hand, the defendant had entirely pure intentions and it was not his intention to insult. On the other, it was not obvious for a reader taking cognizance of the whole content of the articles that the writing in question had an insulting import characterized by anti-Semitism or racism. The discussion of guilt, after all, concerned guilt due to the Jews' rejection of Jesus as the Messiah, not guilt in an ethical or politico-social sense, nor guilt inherent to Jewishness. The Court: 'In their call for conversion, and in the description of the motives for that conversion, the opposite of an anti-Semitic or racist conviction is apparent, not least from the respect with which they speak of the Jewish origin of Jesus and the great abhorrence with which they speak of the persecution of the Jews through the centuries, which they describe as the devil's work.'

The Supreme Court of the Netherlands was not comfortable with this interpretation of the term 'insult' in Section 137e of the Dutch Penal Code.[4] After all, 'from the language in which Section 137e, subsection 1, number 1 of the Dutch Penal Code is phrased, it appears that determining whether a statement is "insulting" to a group of people because of their race and/or faith depends on the nature of that statement and not also on the intentions of the person promulgating the statement'. In addition, a statement to the effect that 'everything that has befallen the Jews, up to the persecution and murder of 6 million Jews by the Nazi regime, is their own fault', is considered insulting in the sense of the aforementioned statutory provision, regardless of the reason(s) why the person who promulgated these statements believes that all this is 'the Jews' own fault'. The Supreme Court reversed the appeal court's acquittal.

WHAT IS AT STAKE?

In cases like the one in hand, one faces a number of conflicts. In the first place, there is a conflict of convictions, a conflict that will presumably not even be resolved by a judicial decision. The Goerees' conviction is that they are free to propagate their faith, even if it entails unintentionally but gravely offending others. Many others are convinced that this is precisely where such freedom runs up against its limits. The two convictions are irreconcilable. Whatever choice one makes as a judge, or as a lawyer trying to put him or herself in the position of a judge, as long as these convictions do not change, a decision will inevitably fail to respect that which is deemed important by at least one of the parties. If the verdict 'guilty' is reached, the sincerely felt need to promulgate the religious conviction is caught in a cleft stick. Acquittal may respect the right to freedom of religion, but the unpleasant consequence of this is that others, who have been deeply offended, and who as a result of the statements feel angry, indignant, fearful or powerless, are told that they should bear those feelings for the sake of other people's right to promulgate their faith. This conflict cannot be circumvented by calling the arguments or standpoints of either of the two parties irrelevant or less important. It will be solved if one of the parties allows itself to be convinced and if emotions subsequently concur with that conviction. (This is extremely implausible in this particular case.) It will also be solved if the parties let themselves be convinced of a compromise: a compromise, for example, in which promulgating and disseminating the religious view in question is allowed, provided that people are safeguarded against coming into contact with it unexpectedly and unwillingly.

A second form of tension arises from the duality of the questions at issue. First, there is the question of who is right in the case of conflicting interpretations of the same situations; second, the question of whether who is right in a case such as this one is actually relevant. I am convinced that the Goerees are putting forward nonsense that calls for strong opposition with arguments; but I am equally convinced that the nonsense of their reading of events provides insufficient reason to fine them or give them a prison sentence. The Goerees have the right to form their own ethical, political and religious views and to act in accordance with them; the circumstance that others consider such views and behaviour as highly reprehensible is in itself insufficient reason to forbid them. The difference between the private sphere, in which everyone can act according to his or her own convictions, and the public sphere, where that is not the case, is something that has come about in the course of time. In the private sphere, autonomy prevails – in the public sphere, limits have been set by the government.

This distinction often leads to a certain tension between what people would find the best solution on the basis of their ethics for the private sphere (the preferred conception of good that can be shared with others and therefore need not necessarily be private ethics) and what can be justified as part of public ethics. I am convinced that it would be morally preferable if there were more listening and less converting; and if emphasis were not placed so much on what divides but on what unites. Finally, I am convinced that the Goerees, in their zeal to convert, have acted in a way that I myself, morally speaking, would not wish to answer for. But does that give one the right to deter those who are eager to convert, and who assume a less than reserved stance, with a fine or a prison sentence? Generally speaking, I do not think that is defensible.

A possible counterargument would be that this outline of the various conflicts arising from a case such as that of the Goerees overlooks the most essential conflict.[5] Is this not, after all, in essence a conflict between religious traditions, or, phrased somewhat differently, a conflict between a religious tradition and what is in many respects a secular philosophy of life in which equal treatment and non-discrimination, also in interpersonal relationships, constitute a new 'faith'? And is it not so that both traditions are claiming their ideas to be true? It is conceivable for both parties to reject the distinction between the private and public sphere so that, in their view, the task of the state is to protect their convictions because they are the right ones. In that case it also becomes apparent that the distinction between a private and a public sphere is not neutral with respect to the various conceptions of ethics, religion and politics. Why, the rhetorical question might be, should adults be given the opportunity to take the wrong path of their own free will? Should the law not compel them to keep to the straight and narrow? Such a position is not in keeping with the ideas of a liberal constitutional state, which by guaranteeing basic rights observes a certain neutrality as regards the truth of convictions relating to religion and life philosophies. But it does make clear that a constitutional and judicial tradition like the Dutch one, which aspires to such neutrality, may find itself under suspicion of bias and a lack of objectivity. I will not pursue this problem further here, because my subject is the objectivity and impartiality of legal decisions within such a constitutional state and not the underlying problem of the objectivity of a religion or a system of political ethics. In the law of the Netherlands, the framework of basic rights and the distinction it makes between private and public sphere is an objective fact constituted as such by law. As I will argue later, this is an objectivity *sui generis*, which is not dependent on the – controversial – objectivity and impartiality of underlying liberal political ethics. It may be that in pluralistic societies only liberal political ethics, maintaining respect for individuals, enable a peaceful solution to fundamental differences of opinion, so that we can designate it in that sense – along with those who give such solutions priority – as the correct political ethics (for this issue, see the essay by A.W. Musschenga). I see the answer to this question as vital, because it can determine the moral acceptability of law. However, what I am concerned with in this chapter is how an objective and unbiased settlement of differences can be possible, given the framework of a state that guarantees its citizens' basic rights and thereby assumes a certain neutrality. The emphasis here lies on a judicial conception of objectivity.

RELEVANT POINTS OF VIEW

One of the intuitive ideas that play a role in the objectivization of one's own position in a conflict is that the individual, personal perspective is confronted with other personal perspectives. In law, this idea is embodied in all kinds of procedural regulations which are intended to promote the representation of the standpoints of all parties involved. Refusal to acknowledge these is seen as a form of bias that stands in the way of objectivity. A first step towards objectivity – if such objectivity is possible at all – is to come to an adequate understanding of the standpoints and arguments of the others.

I shall therefore begin by summarizing a number of viewpoints that are of relevance to the settlement of a conflict such as the Goeree case. I do not guarantee completeness: new arguments in which other factors come to the fore are possible.[6]

I will limit myself to discussing the extent to which the Goerees' conduct is actionable on account of the fact that this conduct has resulted in (serious) offence being given to others. I will leave aside the question of whether the Goerees' conduct could be legally prohibited on the grounds of the physical, psychological or economic damage that it might cause, since this question did not prove relevant in the arguments exchanged during the criminal proceedings.

If we first take a look at the group of people whose feelings have been wounded, the severity of the offence given is a primary factor. This severity depends on the extent as well as on the intensity and duration of the hurt. It can hardly be denied that wounding the feelings of others is wrong *prima facie*, and that a serious affront weighs heavier than a less serious one. In the case in hand, the extent was large. Not only those directly addressed, i.e. members of the Jewish faith and Jews in general, but many others were offended by the Goerees' conduct. This was particularly apparent during the civil proceedings, where, in addition to the Israel Documentation and Information Centre and the Anne Frank Foundation, the Jewish Christian Consultation Foundation and a number of people of non-Jewish extraction acted as claimants. The hurt was also considerable in terms of intensity. To describe the feelings the statements evoked as aggravating would be euphemistic. The feelings – that are liable to vary from person to person – could better be described as astonishment (how can they possibly make such a claim?), abhorrence, disgust, anxiety, powerlessness and also fear. Finally, the hurt, in terms of time, far exceeded a passing irritation. Feinberg proposes that, along with the severity of the hurt, account must be taken of the possibility of an abnormal susceptibility of those whose feelings are wounded. Abnormally heightened sensitivity of the victim makes an affront 'less serious'. There is little reason to assume that the severity of the hurt in the present case should be adjusted downwards. The slate of recent history cannot be wiped clean. If the wounding of feelings is at issue, events that everyone is capable of understanding as having increased susceptibility are relevant. Solicitor General Leijten expressed this as follows in his conclusion to the verdict of the Supreme Court of the Netherlands in the civil action: 'where the treatment of the Jews is concerned, the history of events from 1933–1945 is nearby, whether measured in terms of law, culture, time or place. We must not act as if this were of no consequence. Neither should we regard that as an imperfection in the law. It is inherent in the law.'[7] A susceptibility formed partly as a consequence of abhorrent, perhaps exceptional, events is therefore not the same as an exceptional susceptibility. If one were to blame Catholics or Protestants for the injustices inflicted on them in the past because they adhered to the wrong faith, one would be talking of a less serious hurt because they have not suffered from persecution on the same scale; at least the instances of persecution lie further back in time. The same degree of susceptibility is therefore much more liable to be described as 'abnormal' in their case.

An argument that resembles that of 'abnormal susceptibility', but which in my opinion is a different argument, was put forward by A. Th. van Deursen (Van Deursen 1992: 13). He starts with the proposition that if one accepts that every human being has a right to his or her faith, one must also accept that the 'various basic principles are in conflict with each other'. He goes on to say that it would be absurd if that were not allowed 'because one faith had suffered more than another in the past'. The difference from the argument based on abnormal susceptibility is this: Van Deursen does not need to say (nor does he) that the case in hand concerns abnormal susceptibility. Considering the events, the unusual degree of susceptibility is entirely understandable. However, his argument is that this unusual, yet normal and understandable susceptibility is no reason to restrict the freedom of a faith that happens to oppose the faith that has suffered in history. The difference is subtle, but not insignificant. It is one thing to lay it at the door of others that their feelings are incomprehensible, abnormal and consequently irrelevant, but it is altogether different to say that those feelings are not weighty enough to justify restriction of freedom of religion and the implied right to 'oppose' others who think differently.

A second important factor is whether those whose feelings have been wounded acquiesced in the insult or could reasonably have avoided it. One extreme here is the situation in which the insult is voluntarily sought out or in which the risk of it is consciously run. The other extreme is the situation in which it is reasonably inevitable that people will be confronted with offensive statements (billboards in public places, brochures and pamphlets through the letter-box). The underlying intuition is the adage *volenti non fit iniuria*. Anyone attending a meeting of his own free will while knowing or suspecting that words will be spoken that he is likely to experience as highly offensive is not wronged in any way, because he has consented to being confronted with those statements. In addition, there is the intuition that the severity of the hurt diminishes the less difficult it is to avoid it. In the case in hand, the Goerees' statements were contained in a door-to-door 'gospel' magazine. There was therefore no question of consent to the confrontation. It could be argued that such a method of dissemination does not mean that the efforts that those who received this material through the letter-box had to make to avoid being offended exceeded what was 'reasonable'. Surely one can simply deposit such publications, if one attaches no worth to them, in the waste-paper basket? On the other hand, it can be argued that some people only take such action after having read the contents, however superficially; and that is often more than sufficient to be shocked. Otherwise, everything would have to be consigned to the waste-paper bin unread, and that measure does exceed what is reasonable, because it forces one to discard the information that one does want to read as well.

As distinct from the severity of the offence given, there are a number of additional factors that must at least be considered. Firstly, there is the personal and social importance of the right to choose one's own faith and to promulgate it, interests that are expressed in the freedom of speech and the freedom of religion. It was established during the proceedings that the Goerees were expressing their religious conviction. That conviction may be incoherent (the double guilt concept), offensive and abject to the minds of many, and rest partly on incorrect factual premises (it is certainly not true that only 'converted' Jews were spared), but it is their conviction, and (weighty) reasons are required to discard their personal interest in being able to live in accordance with their faith. This entails respect for them as persons, not respect for their actual convictions. (See the essay by A.W. Musschenga for the difference between respect for the individual and respect for the convictions of an individual.)

Personal autonomy is not the only value at issue here. The plea for freedom of speech has of old been just as much linked to the social benefit expected from the conflict of opinions. Convictions that are incorrect, incoherent or meet with general disapproval are not excepted (J.S. Mill 1859: Ch. 2). There is a right of free speech, not a right of correct speech. And that is not because incorrect views benefit society in any way (they almost by definition do not) but because society is harmed more than it benefits if the authorities decide which views are correct and which are incorrect. Specifically referring to the interdictions in Sections 137c–137f of the Dutch Penal Code, R. de Winter recently provided such an argument (De Winter 1993: 638). He proposes that, however offensive or damaging certain statements may be, it would be wrong to decide to prohibit those statements, because that would be even more detrimental. He adduces four circumstances. Firstly, it is unclear what 'insulting' a particular section of the population actually is. Uncertainty about this makes the fear of a *faux pas* great: 'We need hardly expect any grotesqueries any more, but sublimities are every bit as unlikely. All lines of thought threaten to be nipped in the bud.' A second factor is the danger of arbitrariness. One sometimes reads, as he says, that a copy of *Mein Kampf* has been confiscated. (See, for example, HR 12 March 1987, NJ 1988, 299, in which the Supreme Court nullified an order that rejected a claim to withdraw from circulation a translation of that book.) And yet, for anyone interested, there are still copies on sale 'even at the weekly book market held right in front of the Supreme Court'. (Incidentally, I do not find this part of the argument all that strong; such 'arbitrariness' is inherent in every penal provision. Not everything is traced, and the tracing is also subject to 'priorities'. De Winter should make it clear that a special arbitrariness is at issue here, a conscious, selective application in respect of certain individuals that one – apparently for another reason – wants to 'get hold of'. He proposes that the penal provisions concerned lend themselves to this, not that this kind of arbitrariness actually occurs.)

The third objection is that the interdictions mainly 'affect the small fry', while the racists who know how to package their message 'nicely' (i.e. not by shouting 'foreigners out', but by saying 'our own people first') stay out of harm's way and are in a certain sense even legitimized. The fourth argument, finally, comes down to the fact that 'the most horrible of tortures' is for people to be stopped from sharing their thoughts with others. Things can be shelved for a while, but 'sooner or later the bomb will irrevocably explode. And why should it be limited to words if that happens? I do not find that a comforting prospect. I think I would rather let myself be insulted' (De Winter 1993: 638).

As a whole this reasoning is utilitarian, even rule-utilitarian. There is no reason for exceptions to freedom of speech, not even in exceptional cases.[8] The very possibility of exceptions is considered counterproductive.

Finally, looking at the position of those who offend others, there are two more relevant factors: the difference that can exist between the statement or conviction itself and the form in which it is presented; and the nature of the intentions of the person promulgating the statements concerned.

The first point concerns the following. Anyone examining case law concerning the respective articles in the Dutch Penal Code will come across the most abhorrent statements (see, for example, HR 11 February 1986, NJ 1986, 689, which concerns statements that were interlaced with a number of 'macabre jokes' that I will not repeat here, not even in the interests of a 'factual report'). Sometimes it is simply incomprehensible why certain statements were needed to bring an opinion or conviction into the open, because they constitute no essential part of the content of the conviction but are apparently exclusively included to shock or attract attention. Although we can doubt whether we will always succeed in distinguishing the 'gratuitously offensive form' from the offensive content sufficiently clearly, taking cognizance of a few clear cases will suffice to nuance the rule-utilitarian approach and to feel sympathetic towards Feinberg's observation that 'gratuitously offensive' statements 'derive very little weight from the standard of social utility, and consequently can be rightly restricted by law when the offence they cause is sufficiently serious' (Feinberg 1985: 39). The Goerees, the Court established, had 'through their confrontational manner of writing and the choice of photographic material not created the impression that they were intending to make any concessions for the sake of avoiding a shocking effect and for the sake of increasing their appeal'. Apart from the fact that their conviction itself gave offence (because of the attribution of 'guilt'), the method of presentation was also shocking, as the photographs included depictions of concentration camp prisoners.

The second point that must be taken into consideration is the circumstance of whether or not the person who gave the offence had malicious intentions. Intuitively, someone who makes statements with the sole object of offending others is in a weaker position than someone making such statements in order to convey his or her conviction and who is prepared to put up with the resultant hurt, and maybe also regret it. In the case at hand, it has been established that the Goerees were not intending to insult others.

The muddle of viewpoints that we end up with here provides no solution to our problem. Anyone considering freedom of religion or philosophy of life and freedom of speech to be of prime importance can admit that the arguments pointing towards a restriction of those liberties are significant, but judges that they are not weighty enough to actually tip the balance in that direction. On the other hand, those who hold that seriously wounding the feelings of others is sufficient reason to curtail those rights recognize the weight of those rights but consider them at the same time too minor to be decisive. Between the two extremes lies a whole gamut of solutions, all less abstract than the extremes, because the right to propagate one's own faith or opinion becomes dependent on circumstances, such as the manner of dissemination or the form of the statements.

It is not inconceivable that even those who viewed the Goeree case initially with the most unshakeable conviction will feel some doubt creeping up on them by now. How, in the light of such a diversity of arguments, can one firmly maintain one's position?

If we step back and consider matters from a sufficient distance, even a relativization in which every solution is equally satisfactory within the given margins acquires a certain appeal. A judge, and anyone putting themselves in his or her place, however, faces a choice. I will make such a choice, but before doing so, I wish to consider the question of to what extent such a choice can be objective in the context of the law, or at least increase the chances of an intersubjective acceptability.

OBJECTIVITY OR SUBJECTIVITY?

What objectivization can be expected here within the framework of legal proceedings?

To start with, it does not go without saying that we can expect to be able to provide the norms, principles and values that are expressed in positive law with an objective basis. Much depends on the notion of objectivity that one applies. For some, an objective judgement is characterized by the fact that it represents a state of affairs that exists as a kind of reality apart from any (human) perspective. In so far as the law is concerned, such a view is expressed in certain variants of thinking on natural law in which, in addition to man-made law (positive law), there are norms and values that exist independently of human decisions of will, and that can be recognized in human nature.

It is doubtful whether such views, in which norms and values are attributed a real existence, can be refuted in the strictest sense of the word (Nagel 1986: 143–9). We cannot pin it on the adherents to this view that their position is inherently contradictory as a consequence of the assumption of a normative reality. For Nagel, it can acquire a certain plausibility if one succeeds in undermining the anti-realistic arguments. Subsequently, an attempt could be made by means of ethical argument to identify ethical reasons that are valid (exist) independently of any human perspective. For example, he himself considers that pain is bad, objectively speaking. People have reason to stop pain whenever possible, whatever their preferences. If Nagel says that when he has a headache he has an objective reason to put an end to that pain, that objective reason is the 'badness of pain'. The fact that he also has another reason for taking measures, i.e. that he does not enjoy headaches, does not detract from that.

I doubt whether such a standpoint is intelligible, but wish to let the discussion rest here. Instead, I would like to say something about the importance of this standpoint for the debate on normative questions. There are two reasons for this. Firstly, the concept of objectivity in question seems to be of little or no consequence for the daily practice of legal (and ethical) reasoning (Waldron 1992: 158–87). The 'knowledge' of normative facts or a normative reality is only communicable in terms of a historically developed language and the conceptualizations it is based on, which need not necessarily be the most apt for expressing the assumed reality. Moreover, adherents to this kind of objectivism are confronted with other opinions, not seldom from their own camp. Thus the characteristics of the cognizing subject still become relevant at the epistemological level. This gives rise to the question in what way reliable knowledge can be acquired. There is no reason to exclude the possibility of short-sightedness, self-interest, misperception and social pressure also playing a role. For the objectivist, these kinds of factors form a pre-eminent explanation for the existence of differences of opinion. An objectivist could, for example, say that it is true that the Goerees are free to propagate their religious conviction because people own this right by nature. The circumstance that others think differently about that does not refute the speaker's claim. His claim of truth means that those with other convictions are, in his opinion, labouring under misapprehensions. But at the same time, the clash of convictions is not without its problems; because it is incumbent on the objectivist to indicate how correct true understanding is to be distinguished from a fallacy. He cannot argue in favour of his own normative judgement by pointing to its truth, or by referring to the untruth of his opponent's judgement. *If* he provides arguments, it will bring him nearer to those who may not be objectivists, but who do allow room for well-considered choices in a normative context.[9]

If this observation is correct, there is every reason to search for another conception of objectivity that does justice to the claim of correctness contained in every normative judgement, but is not founded on 'the view from nowhere'. The room for that exists. The notion of objectivity is a human construction. There is no reality that forces us to recognize a certain conception of objectivity. Even if values and norms existed apart from any human perspective, that reality would still not force us to see it as normative. Definitions of objectivity depend on human decisions (Glastra van Loon 1980: 138).

There are also other reasons that can be given for turning to a different definition of objectivity. Firstly, it is not very satisfactory to end up with a purely subjectivist or intersubjectivist view in which norms and values are made or broken according to personal preferences, whether shared or not. We do not usually assume that something is lawfully or ethically correct because it has our preference. That is simply not a tenable standpoint in our practical reasoning. We claim our decision to be correct (at least, we claim that this decision is not incorrect). We attempt to justify our preference by pointing to something outside ourselves that makes the decision a good one. This in itself still proves nothing. Adherents to the 'error theory' will confront us with the assertion that this claim can never be verified. For them, practical argumentation is not a method with which to arrive at correct understandings (these do not exist), but a method to convince others to adopt our standpoint. Meanwhile, however, the error theorist who believes that the claim of truth (correctness or validity) associated with normative judgements is based on an illusion because no normative judgement can ever be true, also assumes a 'view from nowhere'. After all, he believes that normative judgements cannot make any claim to truth. But with that he has not demonstrated the impossibility of using a notion of objectivity that makes the claim to truth attached to normative judgements comprehensible, and also makes it possible for the correctness of certain judgements to be established.

The other reason is specific to the law. It is essential in law that purely subjective judgement be banished as far as possible. All law presupposes that the one appointed to settle conflicts does so at least partly on the basis of norms that are not the personal creation of the decider. If law were totally dependent on individual judgement, it would not be law. It could not serve to harmonize human conduct. By that I do not mean that there are no elements of law that are strongly subject to the influence of subjective judgement and as a result make a fragmented impression, but that this phenomenon cannot extend through the entire legal system without undermining its *raison d'être*. If everything could be left to the judgement of the autonomous individual in consultation with other autonomous individuals, no law would be necessary to coordinate human behaviour. But ethical or social debate does not always lead to shared convictions, and therefore law, or some equivalent mechanism, is necessary to achieve coordination. It can only do so, however, if it has a certain degree of objectivity.

THE LEGAL CONSTRUCTION OF OBJECTIVITY

The question of objectivity is raised again, but now in a slightly different form. Is law, as a human construction, a recognizable objective fact? Here, too, we come up against the phenomenon that some lawyers indeed speak of the law as if it were an object that existed independently of the perspectives of the cognizing subject and immediately foisted itself on that subject, as it were.

A common view on legal objectivity

I will begin with a view in which the objectivity of the law is sketched in this way. In that common, but not undisputed view, the judicial perspective is central. The judge is bound by law. For the judge, the law is a heteronomous measure, a measure that is not subject to choice but is enforced from outside. A judge who follows the law is objective in that sense. Problems of objectivity arise when the law is unclear and allows diverse interpretations (which, according to some, is nearly always the case). Problems also occur when statutory provisions contradict each other, or, through evaluative terms, indicate that judges must form their own judgement and thereby will have to draw on their ability to form judgements. For instance, there are cases in which the fulfilment of an agreement is made dependent on reason and fairness, and in which an obligation to pay damages is made dependent on whether or not the person causing the damage has acted in contravention of that which is 'proper in social intercourse'. Another example is the question of whether the action of the Goerees amounted to promulgating an insulting statement in the sense of Section 137e of the Dutch Penal Code.

Wiarda outlines a development in which this last situation in particular is occurring with increasing frequency and is attracting more and more attention. He insists on objectivization (Wiarda 1988: 105–7): 'Precisely where his autonomy appears greatest, he will for that reason have to make the most effort to make his decisions in accordance with the objective norms, principles and legal convictions applicable in the society in which he lives and works, and from which he derives his authority.'

What factors can contribute to the objectivization of legal judgement? The factors include legal principles, custom, the convictions of justice among the Dutch populace, and the social and personal interests involved in a case. The principles are found by 'investigating the guiding thoughts on which the given legal system is based, as made positive in legislation and case law, partly on the basis of the elements in or in addition to it that impose themselves on us with immediate obviousness from our sense of justice or moral convictions' (Wiarda 1988: 108–9).

All this, however, is not sufficient for a full objectivization. Legal principles can point in different directions (ibid.: 111). Personal or social interests can constitute reason to deviate from principles (ibid.: 113) and a common conviction of justice is usually lacking. The judge is responsible for a personal prioritization of these objective factors, in so far as present. This process of consideration is not entirely subjective. Wiarda sees in what he calls the comparison method 'a method that reduces uncertainty and can lead to a method of judgement that is more than an intuitive choice and that reinforces the objective, or, if you like, "transsubjective" slant of the judicial interpretation in this area' (ibid.: 132).

Applied to the question of whether the Goerees have made themselves guilty of a 'public insult', this method would mean presupposing a situation in which there is a clear-cut case of insult and a situation in which that is clearly not the case. If the two were compared, relevant differences would become clear that could serve as criteria in case of doubt. The method ensures that new solutions will follow on from already existing convictions, and makes argument possible. An example of the application of this method in the Goeree case would start out with two clear-cut situations. Firstly, a statement made on the basis of one's own religious faith (or philosophy of life) at which others take offence definitely does not constitute any 'public insult' if the others have 'voluntarily' come into contact with it. In the second situation, the same statement is definitely a case of 'public insult' if the statement was not motivated by religion or philosophy of life, and those taking offence at the statement were confronted with it unwillingly. In case of doubt – for example, if an involuntary confrontation with a religious conviction were concerned – a comparison of the two situations could lead to or at least facilitate a responsible decision. The underlying reason is the judge's endeavour to pronounce his judgement in such a way that it not only 'satisfies his own sense of justice, but is at the same time responsible *vis-à-vis* the sense of justice of the circle it is intended for' (Wiarda 1988: 105).

The method is of heuristic relevance; it draws attention to differences and similarities. It is also significant with regard to legitimization, because it frames the decision in the totality of existing convictions. However, the method dictates no solution. Ultimately, the decision is a matter of the judge's personal appreciation (ibid.: 142).

What can be said about this view of objectivity? I see it as being characterized by a strong duality of objective factors, on the one hand, and subjective preferences, on the other. The picture evoked is one of a legal reality (consisting of the law, legal principles, personal and social interests, etc.) that can be recognized, without perspectives, by the judge. Where this objective fact runs up against its limits, the judge can do nothing other than follow his personal judgement.

A hermeneutic perspective

A hermeneutic perspective would take the edge off this contrast because the cognizing subject is given a place in it. However, at the same time, one could add that it conceals a threat to the unity of justice, and thus to justice itself (Van Zaltbommel 1993: particularly Ch. IV). One cannot allow the personal perspective to prevail in determining whether or not the Goerees are guilty of a public insult. The problem after all is that there are too many personal perspectives: on the meaning of statutes and existing case law; on the applicable legal principles; on the personal and social interests that are at issue; and on the weight of each of those factors. How, amid such a chaos of personal perspectives, can an 'objectivity' of the law come about which would allow the replacement of the cognizing subject with any other, without the result being influenced?

For the hermeneutic approach, the solution lies in intersubjectivity. If this is to be a real solution, the intersubjectivity must be actual and not hypothetical. After all, the fact that we should all arrive at certain convictions does not solve the problem of the chaos of subjective opinions as long as we have not actually arrived at those convictions.

The turn towards the notion of intersubjectivity thus understood evokes a number of questions. Firstly, whether law can be based on a consensus, and whether the development of law can be left to the development of that consensus; secondly, the question of to which group of people the intersubjectivity is geared and in what way it can be ensured that the intersubjectivity in the law is not the intersubjectivity of a limited group but that of all those involved.

I will limit myself to a general discussion of the two questions in the order indicated above. More can be said about the problems raised than I will say here, but I hope the following will give a sufficient impression of the direction in which I feel it is necessary to look for the solution.

As far as the first point is concerned, there is, of course, also a certain consensus in a multiform society like ours. For example, there are no pleas for having manslaughter and murder removed from the Criminal Code, and the fact that they are conceivable does not detract from an actually existing consensus, and therefore need not give cause for concern. There are also cases in which the existing consensus is spontaneously renewed. But it is unrealistic to assume that every aspect in our present legal system is supported by consensus, and that we should be able to leave the development of the law to the socio-legal debate. The discourse does not invariably lead to common solutions, to say the least. What we need is a form of objectivity that is *designed* by authoritative bodies especially charged to do so.

OBJECTIVITY AS CONSTRUCTION

It is a function of the law to create objectivity where it is lacking. Legislative bodies that are bound by special procedures establish binding norms that make it henceforth possible to speak of a certain objective correctness of legal judgements. As we saw earlier, they will not be one hundred per cent successful in this. A law may, for example, be unclear, or contain an essential contradiction, but that does not detract from the fact that much of what is said is indeed clear and does lay a foundation for objectivity. From a personal perspective, acceptance of this construction of objectivity obviously remains dependent on a choice. Apart from the occasional anarchist, people usually agree that a society benefits from this form of authority. Therefore, there is apparently not so much choice after all. Legal objectivity is based on a large but not total consensus on the necessity of authority.

The construction of objectivity as outlined here can nevertheless only succeed if the bodies entrusted with authority do not make their decisions entirely arbitrarily. Without a minimum of cogency, willingness to accept this form of objectivity would be jeopardized. The deciding body will therefore have to take account of the existing viewpoints in a society. That 'will have to' can be variously interpreted. On the one hand, there is the instrumental reading: the authoritative bodies 'have to', because they will otherwise not succeed in maintaining a law that offers a basis for objective judgements. On the other hand, there is the moral reading: because law concerns everyone, the acceptability of that law demands that the standpoints of everyone are taken into account. Also, the deciding authoritative body does not have full discretion. It will have to objectify its judgement.

A potential cause for concern is that the instrumental reading is presumably reconcilable with great injustice. The solution to that problem is not that one demands right away that authoritative bodies start deciding on the basis of ethics, because, given the differences of opinion on the subject, the question is 'which ethics?' There may be a consensus that offers an ethical basis and can serve as the point of departure for the considerations, but often enough there is not. The criminal court that had to settle the Goeree case was indeed able to draw on a certain consensus (for example, the importance of basic rights), but could not derive from it the answer to the question of how far that right should extend in this case, because that was precisely the point that was disputed. Nor can we say, however, that the judge can decide as he pleases. The question is therefore what should be his guiding principle given the diversity in ethical convictions that are all claimed to be correct.

I previously pointed out that the law usually contains certain guarantees to ensure that everyone gets a say and can present his or her view on the case. All the same, the fact that the various standpoints, if everything proceeds as it should, can be heard, is not enough in itself to ensure that sufficient account will be taken of those standpoints. In other words, it ought to be possible to specify a kind of method or way of thinking that would allow taking up the standpoint of an 'impartial spectator', while one must avoid lapsing into a strictly utilitarian approach in which the right to propagate one's own religious faith in a certain way (or the prohibition on doing so) ensues from an analysis of the social costs and benefits. The utilitarian viewpoint is too impartial and cannot prevent personal values from being totally subordinated to the common good.

I do not think that a strict method of impartiality exists in legal thought, although much (Western) law contains elements that contribute to allowing the various perspectives of involved parties to be heard: for instance, basic rights, the principle of equality, and the consideration of interests that play such a central role in many areas of the law. In so far as one can speak of a method, it is characterized by three basic principles: the pursuit of a universalization of legal judgements; the aim to maintain coherence; and the search for a reasonable compromise. I will say something about each of these three factors.

UNIVERSALIZATION, COHERENCE AND COMPROMISES

The requirement of universalization first and foremost means that legal judgement is based on general judgements, i.e. judgements from which proper names and other uniquely specifying descriptions are excluded. That demand must guarantee that Goeree is not sentenced because he is Goeree, or because it was *his* religious faith that gave offence: he can only be sentenced because his conduct evinces certain characteristics that render that conduct punishable. Both the judgement that anyone may propagate his or her religious faith and the judgement that this may exclusively be permitted as long as it does not seriously offend others, are universalized in this sense. Universalization means that reasons are provided for legal judgements. The requirement of coherence means that these reasons must also be applied consistently.

Coherent universalization stems subjectivity. It is no longer the case that everything is possible. However, this first step does not take us far enough (even if it asks more than can be guaranteed in an existing legal system (Brouwer 1992: 178–92)). It does not exclude the possibility of certain views being totally discounted.

A second step in the process of universalization could be for the judge to put himself in the position of the parties involved. The question is then 'How would I consider being deeply offended by the way in which others propagate their religion?' And also, 'How would I feel if I were not allowed to propagate my own religion?' And yet in this case a step would be taken – although it can never be entirely avoided – that should not be taken because it would make the personal (political or moral) perspective of the judge decisive. Such an approach does not square with the picture that many judges have of themselves. In the words of one judge, 'One's political views play no role in one's judgement as a judge. The general impression may be different, but the law is quite objective in this country. Your own opinion is irrelevant. I come from a fairly orthodox Catholic background, and I still largely adhere to that body of ideas. As a consequence, I do not regard divorce as an obvious, natural thing to do. Yet I spent two years in the family chamber and passed hundreds of divorces. The profession entails that I do not get personally involved. I have not found that to be a problem' (Willems 1991).

Such complete impartiality seems an incoherent notion. The question is how a comprehensible version would look. An ideal situation would be one in which solutions were chosen that can count on the actual agreement of all. That is not possible if there is no shared ground that can form the basis of objective decisions which the involved parties also see as correct. What can a judge who strives to be unbiased tell the parties? He could refer to one of the primary tasks of the law: the regulation of human behaviour in the interests of a peaceful society. He could reason as follows: conflicts can evoke violence; to avoid that, and given the irreconcilable differences of opinion, a certain degree of compliance is necessary, which means that a compromise is the appropriate way. I consider the conclusion yielded by this reasoning to be a correct one. Yet, I would prefer other premises for various reasons. Firstly, one can argue with good grounds that if the decision is a correct one, the Government may not, in principle, yield to any violence from those who strongly disagree with the decision. For example, a 'hostile audience' is not normally considered a good reason to limit the right of others to hold a demonstration. Only if serious disorderliness cannot be expected to be curbed by other means could peace-keeping prevail over the right to demonstrate. (In this context, it can be remarked *obiter dictum* that insulting a section of the population is a violation of civil order pursuant to Section 137e (Stolwijk 1988: 119 ff.).) On the other hand, the compromise itself could threaten the peace. If it is only a question of avoiding disturbance of the peace by a large number of dissatisfied parties, it becomes important to take account of the convictions of as many people as possible rather than taking account of as many convictions as possible. I am not saying that the necessity to do so never exists. The point is that it depicts the 'emergency' situation as the normal one.

So why is a compromise the appropriate way? In my opinion, because it is the only way, in the absence of a consensus, of recognizing the equality of legal subjects as much as possible. Remaining convinced of being morally right would mean treating others unfairly. They, too, have a right to their convictions and interests being taken into consideration and allowed for, in so far as possible, in the final decision. One can trust that one is ethically right and attempt to convince others. Forcing one's conviction of being right on others with the aid of the law goes too far. I can obviously not deny that this standpoint also betrays a certain bias, but that bias is as small as it can be, and is certainly smaller than when the position of some is entirely determined by the views of others.

I am aware that much remains to be done to specify this rather intuitive sketch of the compromise as the most impartial solution. Yet, this notion cannot be brought into discredit in the way in which Dworkin has done (Dworkin 1986: 176 ff.). His argument suggests that a compromise is a nonsensical construction that no one can assume responsibility for. In the case of ethical differences of opinion about abortion, for example, a compromise could mean that abortion by women born in even years would be punishable and by women born during uneven years would not be. Indeed, if that were a typical example of a compromise, one would do best to dismiss the notion. It is not the kind of compromise that can increase the acceptability of decisions. What is going wrong here is that a coherent universalization is missing. Neither supporters nor opponents can see why a woman's year of birth should be a relevant reason for a moral and legal judgement on abortion. That is because in this 'compromise' equal weight is attributed to their convictions, but not to the reasons for those convictions. In that sense, the example is illustrative. It shows that a compromise can only be acceptable to the adherents of the divergent standpoints if the reasons for those standpoints are also taken into account in that compromise.

A COMPROMISE IN THE GOEREE CASE

The proof of the pudding is in the eating. What does a compromise look like that considers the reasons of both the advocates and the opponents of punishing Goeree?

The compromise is based on the viewpoints that were previously set forth. The most central of these are that everyone has a right to propagate his or her own religion or philosophy of life (and has a right to freedom of speech), and that it is wrong *prima facie* to offend others because of their race, religion or philosophy of life. If one were to give one of these values priority under all circumstances, the position of some of those involved would be fully subordinated to the convictions and feelings of others. In one case, the limits of the freedom of religion and speech would be totally determined by the circumstance of whether others feel deeply offended or not. In the other case, those who are involved in exercising these rights would be without any protection against that. A compromise would have to leave room for propagating one's own religion (which requires 'the promulgation of statements'), while at the same time offering a certain degree of protection to groups that are insulted by those statements because of race, religion or philosophy of life. The attention is then necessarily shifted to concomitant circumstances. The intentions of the party making the statements become relevant, as well as the severity of the insult, the form in which the statements were made, the method of dissemination, whether the confrontation with the statements was voluntary or not, etc. Those factors do not all point in the same direction in the present case. It is in Goeree's favour that it was not his intention to insult others. On the other hand, he confronted others with shocking statements against their will. The method of dissemination demands more of those who wish to be spared the statements in question than is reasonable. It can also be said to Goeree's disadvantage that the form he chose was gratuitously offensive. It is true that in the first instance the content of his religion was already sufficient to deeply hurt others. Nevertheless, the presentation of that conviction was not free from sensationalism. Given these circumstances, a compromise might entail that the right to propagate one's religion or opinion under the following two circumstances can in any case be limited in order to avoid insulting others: firstly, when the chosen form is unnecessarily offensive; secondly, when those others are confronted with the seriously offensive statements against their will or without their having been able to avoid such with reasonable means.

Against the background of the individual ethical opinion, this could be termed a half-and-half solution. It is to be hoped that the parties concerned will also see the value of that 'half-and-halfness', and that the decision will be accepted by all and not just by some as a decision that, given the ethical differences of opinion, is the most defensible solution for all those involved. If the attempt to do so succeeds, the edges will be taken off the conflict existing between them – which does not mean that a certain tension will cease to exist between one's own ethical judgement and that based on public ethics guided by impartiality.

For the judge, this may imply another relationship of tension, because the compromise must be reconcilable with applicable law. It seems to me that the compromise outlined above does not agree perfectly with Section 137e of the Dutch Penal Code, which makes no distinction between content and form of the insulting statements, nor between various methods of dissemination. The introduction of these refinements would lead to a restrictive interpretation of the section. I think that the need for a compromise provides grounds for that. Those grounds, however, cannot be freely weighed against the reasons that argue for a judge to resign himself to the decisions of the legislator, because it would mean a denial of his authority. If the decision of an authority only had to be followed if that decision was, all things considered, deserving of preference, there would be no question of authority. That does not exclude a weighing out process.[10] Certainly, there appear to be no preponderant objections to circumventing the law if it is clear that this will meet with general agreement. That would hardly constitute a threat to the objectivity of the law. Objectivity is threatened, however, if opinions start diverging, as has happened in the case at hand. In such cases, there are no apparent reasons why a judge, instead of maintaining a given 'objectivity', should replace it with a new one.

NOTES

1 Section 137e now also makes it punishable to insult a section of the population because of 'heterosexual or homosexual orientation', as well as to incite hatred or discrimination against people, or acts of violence against the person or goods of people because of sex or heterosexual or homosexual orientation.

2 District Court Zwolle, 9 October 1986, NJ 1987, 524.

3 Court of Appeal Arnhem, 29 May 1987, NJ 1987, 816.

4 Supreme Court of the Netherlands 18 October 1988, NJ 1989, 476; with note G.E.M.

5 At this point, I will not discuss a third form of conflict which can occur in the potential field of tension between what positive law (in this case Section 137e of the Dutch Penal Code and the principles involved here) requires of the judge and what this judge sees as the best solution (ethically speaking) on the basis of arguments.

6 The overview is based both on the arguments that were exchanged in the legal proceedings and the observations of Feinberg on the question of whether, and if so when, wounding the feelings of others can constitute grounds for the Government to instigate criminal proceedings. See Feinberg 1985. There is a large consensus as to what the relevant factors are. Almost all those mentioned by Feinberg occur in some way or another in case law. In itself, that is a sign of a certain intersubjectivity. Disagreement mainly arises if it is a matter of determining the weight of these factors.

7 HR 5 June 1987, NJ 1988, 702.

8 Except when the statements directly lead to violence; De Winter makes an exception for the so-called 'fighting words'. For the 'fighting words' doctrine, see Feinberg 1985: 226 ff.

9 It is possible that the objectivist will close the debate with the pronouncement 'that is just how things happen to be'. Debate may also be excluded from the outset. Glastra van Loon points out that the combination of claims to universality and actual social barriers (which hinder the communicability of judgements) creates social polarization (Glastra van Loon 1980: 151).

10 Apart from cases in which the constitution leaves such a consideration to judges, one might consider the correction of apparent legislative mistakes, the removal of contradictions, and the correction of extreme forms of injustice.

REFERENCES

Brouwer, P. W. (1992) 'Over coherentie in recht', *Nederlands Tijdschrift voor Rechtsfilosofie en Rechtstheorie* 3: 178–92.

De Winter, R. E. (1993) 'Straffeloos beledigen', *Nederlands Juristenblad* 17: 638.

Dworkin, R. (1986) *Law's Empire*, London: Fontana Press.

Feinberg, J. (1985) *Offense to Others*, New York: Oxford University Press.

Glastra van Loon, J. F. (1980) *De eenheid van het handelen. Opstellen over recht en filosofie*, Amsterdam: Boom.

Mill, J. S. (1859) 'On liberty', in Gertrude Himmelfarb (ed.) (1974) *On the Liberty of Thought and Discussion*, Harmondsworth: Penguin

Nagel, T. (1986) *The View from Nowhere*, New York: Oxford University Press.

Stolwijk, S. A. M. (1988) 'De zaak Goeree, ofwel " . . . behoudens ieders verantwoordelijkheid volgens de wet" ', *Ars Aequi* 37: 119–27.

Van Deursen, A. Th. (1992) Interview in *VU-Magazine*, 21 April 1992.

Van Zaltbommel, L. K. (1993) *De betekenis van het recht als systeem*, Zwolle: W. E. J. Tjeenk Willink.

Waldron, J. (1992) 'The irrelevance of moral objectivity', in R. P. George (ed.) *Natural Law Theory. Contemporary Essays*, Oxford: Clarendon Press.

Wiarda, G. (1988) *Drie typen van rechtsvinding*, 2nd edit., Zwolle: W.E.J. Tjeenk Willink.

Willems, J. H. M. (1991) Interview in *Vrij Nederland*, 2 November 1991: 53.

INDEX